Oxford**basics**

INTRODUCTION
TO TEACHING ENGLISH

Oxford Basics series

Presenting New Language
Simple Listening Activities
Simple Reading Activities
Simple Writing Activities
Simple Speaking Activities
Classroom English
Intercultural Activities
Teaching Grammar
Cross-curricular Activities
Activities Using Resources

Oxford Basics for Children series

Vocabulary Activities
Listen and Do
Storytelling
English through Music

See the Oxford University Press ELT website at
http://www.oup.com/elt
for further details

Oxford**basics**

Introduction to Teaching English

JILL HADFIELD

CHARLES HADFIELD

OXFORD

UNIVERSITY PRESS

OXFORD
UNIVERSITY PRESS

Great Clarendon Street, Oxford OX2 6DP

Oxford University Press is a department of the University of Oxford.
It furthers the University's objective of excellence in research, scholarship,
and education by publishing worldwide in

Oxford New York

Auckland Cape Town Dar es Salaam Hong Kong Karachi
Kuala Lumpur Madrid Melbourne Mexico City Nairobi
New Delhi Shanghai Taipei Toronto

With offices in

Argentina Austria Brazil Chile Czech Republic France Greece
Guatemala Hungary Italy Japan South Korea Poland Portugal
Singapore Switzerland Thailand Turkey Ukraine Vietnam

OXFORD and OXFORD ENGLISH are registered trade marks of
Oxford University Press in the UK and in certain other countries

ISBN: 978 0 19 441975 8

Printed and bound by Eigal S.A. in Portugal

ACKNOWLEDGEMENTS

*The authors and publisher are grateful to those who have given
permission to reproduce the following extracts and adaptations of
copyright material:*

p.143 Extracts from A Common European Framework of
Reference for Languages: Learning, Teaching, Assessment ©
Council of Europe; p.163–173 Grammar terminology entries
and Glossary entries from Oxford Learner's Grammar by John
Eastwood © Oxford University Press 2005; p.163–169 Glossary
entries from Learning and Teaching English by Cora Lindsay and
Paul Knight © Oxford University Press 2006; p.163–169 Glossary
entries from Success in English Teaching by Paul Davies and Eric
Pearse © Oxford University Press 2000

*The publishers wish to thank the following for their kind permission to
reproduce photographs:*

Alamy p.67 (Hotel/Barry Lewis), (umbrellas in the rain/William
S. Kuta); OUP p.67 (hotel room, beach umbrella, mountains,
dead fish)

Illustrations by:

Adrian Barclay pp.11, 15, 16, 23, 25, 38, 41, 50, 51, 54, 56, 62, 97,
112, 124, 160; Heather Clarke pp.6, 141, 148, 154

Cover image courtesy

Getty Images/Jack Hollingsworth/Photodisc

Hutia te rito o te harakeke
Mai wai te komako e ko?
E patai atu ahau ki a koe,
He aha te mea nui o te ao?
He tangata, he tangata, he tangata.

Take away the heart of the flax bush
and where will the bellbird sing?
Let me ask you,
What is the most important thing in this world?
It is people, it is people, it is people.

Traditional Maori saying

Contents

Introduction   1

Unit 1   **Some basic principles**   3

Unit 2   **Focus on language**   9
- **2.1** The structure of a language lesson   10
- **2.2** Focus on grammar   18
- **2.3** Focus on functions   32
- **2.4** Focus on vocabulary   45
- **2.5** Focus on pronunciation   58

Unit 3   **Focus on skills**   71
- **3.1** The structure of a skills lesson   72
- **3.2** Focus on listening   77
- **3.3** Focus on reading   91
- **3.4** Focus on speaking   105
- **3.5** Focus on writing   116

Unit 4   **Putting it together**   133
- **4.1** Planning lessons and lesson sequences   134
- **4.2** Review, assessment, and remedial work   140
- **4.3** Classroom management   145

Appendices   157
- Lesson materials   157
- Glossary   163
- Grammar terminology table   170
- Further reading   174

Introduction

This book is for teachers who are learning to teach English either on an initial teacher training course, or beginning their teaching career. It is a little different from other teacher training manuals in two ways.

It is written for all beginning teachers of ELT but bears in mind the needs of many of the world's teachers who do not have easy access to equipment such as photocopiers, cassette recorders, DVD players, computers, libraries of resource books — or who may not even have a course book. The techniques and activities in the lesson plans in this book do not assume that you have this equipment in your school or classroom. Instead, the focus is on classroom techniques and activities that use home-produced materials and resources — or even no materials at all. This does not mean that if you work in a hi-tech school this book is not for you, it is simply that we firmly believe that lo-tech is not second best. Many simple techniques and home-produced materials can bring colour, life, warmth, and laughter into the classroom in a way that books and equipment cannot: all teachers can benefit from using them!

The second way it is different is in the way it is organized. We have vivid memories of our own teacher training courses and watch our trainees now going through the same process: So many new things to learn! So much information! How can I put it all together? Trainees read books on listening, vocabulary, classroom management — and wonder how to weave all these different insights together into a whole lesson. We decided to approach the problem in a different direction — by structuring this book around a series of whole lessons which are described in detail, with comments on key points. We hope that this whole-to-part approach will complement the part-to-whole approach of most methodology books.

The book has a simple structure. There is a brief introduction, outlining some basic principles behind the teaching approach in the book, and a conclusion with practical suggestions for planning lessons and managing classes. In between are sections on different types of lesson, e.g. a grammar lesson, a writing lesson, etc. Each section contains an introduction followed by two sample lessons with comments. The two lessons are designed to contrast with each other to show different teaching possibilities.

You can use the book in different ways. You might like to use it as pre-course reading, to give you an idea of what teaching an English lesson might be like and what issues are important. In this way, reading the book will be like being invited into a classroom to watch some lessons taught by a teacher who gives you some explanations about what she is doing and why she has chosen that particular way of doing it. You may use it during your course, and if you are doing teaching practice, you may like to try out some of the lessons as an alternative to teaching from a course book: this will give you practice in making your own materials—or even teaching with few or no materials. The comments in the lesson plans will give you practical hints on how to prepare materials, how to organize groups etc., as well as insights into the aims and methodological considerations behind the activities. If you are already teaching, the book may give you some support with lessons, techniques, and activities that you can use or adapt.

Whatever your situation and however you use the book, we hope it will help you begin to find a way through the maze of new ideas and support you in your new venture. Good luck!

Please note that sometimes the teacher is referred to as 'he' and sometimes as 'she'—simply to reflect the fact that teachers may be men or women. Similarly, 'student' and 'learner' are used interchangeably, with no intended significance.

1 Some basic principles

Let's begin with what is most important in any classroom: the people.

Learners are all very different. They differ in obvious ways: age, gender, nationality, language level, and personality. But they also differ in less immediately obvious ways. Their attitudes in the classroom are affected by their motivations, their needs, their educational and cultural backgrounds, and their learning styles and personalities.

Motivation and needs

People may be learning English because of some external reason or **extrinsic** motivation: for their career or for their studies, in which case they may have an examination to pass. Other learners may be learning English for pleasure, for socializing and conversation, or simply out of interest in an English-speaking country and culture. These students, whose motivation comes from within themselves, have an **intrinsic** motivation. Some students may not be motivated, but be learning English because they have to. Students will have different needs and wants depending on their reasons for learning English. Some may want a focus on grammar and exam practice, while others are more likely to be interested in vocabulary and conversation than exam skills.

Educational and cultural background

According to their educational background and culture, learners will have differing expectations of what an English lesson will be like. In some countries, language lessons are based on grammar, translation, and reading activities, whereas in others, the focus is more on speaking, listening, and communicating than on grammar. Some learners may not have learnt their English in a classroom at all, but may have visited or lived in an English-speaking country and learnt the language by picking it up through conversation. Previous language-learning experience will shape what a learner expects from their English class, and will determine which areas they most need to work on to improve their language **skills**.

Learning styles

Another important learner difference to take into account is learning style. Different people rely on different senses to help them learn. You may have a/an:

- **auditory learning style**: learning best when using listening stimuli such as spoken language, music, or sounds
- **visual learning style**: learning best when using visual material such as pictures, diagrams, or writing
- **kinaesthetic learning style**: learning best when using movement.

Traditional education is biased towards a visual learning style, but there are lots of activities you can do (and will discover in this book) to cater for all learning styles. As you develop as a teacher, catering for different learning styles will be something you become more and more efficient at doing.

Learning style is also dependent on personality. Learners can be extrovert or introvert: sociable or shy. The more extrovert learners will enjoy speaking activities, and the more introvert ones will be more comfortable working on their own with a quiet **activity** like reading. They may be impulsive risk takers, willing to try out new language immediately, or more cautious, reflective types who need time to feel confident with new language before using it. They may prefer to 'absorb' the language, picking it up subconsciously by listening and reading, or they may prefer more conscious analysis of the grammar.

What makes a good learner?

We have seen that learners learn in different ways — is one way better than the others? There is no one 'right' way to learn a language — but there are some qualities that many successful learners share. They are highly motivated: they have a clear sense of direction and know what they want to achieve. They have an urge to find things out for themselves by asking questions or looking things up. They are willing to 'have a go' and try out new language, and they are self-directed, taking responsibility for their own learning.

Teaching styles

Just as learners have different learning styles, teachers have different teaching styles. A teacher may be a methodical planner with a clear, organized teaching style or more of an improviser, with a flexible, responsive style. Some teachers are natural entertainers with larger-than-life personalities, some have a calm and sympathetic classroom presence. Some teachers have an authoritative teaching style, while others see themselves as helpers or 'facilitators', encouraging learners to discover things for themselves. Teaching style obviously depends also on personality — whether you are extrovert or introvert, analytic and logical or intuitive and responsive, down-to-earth or imaginative, but the teaching role you adopt in the classroom will also depend on your beliefs about teaching and learning. Do you think of knowledge as something passed from teacher to learner or something that learners can be encouraged to discover themselves with help from the teacher?

What makes a good teacher?

In general, it is best to try to achieve a balance. An exuberant personality may neglect learners' needs; a quieter teacher may be more responsive but also less colourful and memorable. A careful planner may lack the spontaneity and flexibility necessary to respond to learners' needs, while improvised lessons may be chaotic or lack clarity and focus. There are times when you need to explain and give information to your students and other times when you encourage them to discover for themselves. The balance you aim for may be different according to your students' needs — and ultimately this attention to the needs and wants of your students, and willingness to adapt to meet them, is what makes a good teacher.

It is important for you to find a teaching style which is right for you and that you feel comfortable with. It is impossible to teach in a way you feel instinctively to be wrong, but you also have a duty to your learners; to respect their individuality and to offer a range of teaching techniques and activities to suit different learning styles. In practice this means what we call 'principled eclecticism'. Eclecticism means that you can pick and choose techniques and classroom activities, instead of sticking closely to a 'method'. However, merely picking techniques at random without some reason for choosing them would lead to chaos! We must have some guiding principles behind our approach to teaching. These principles will decide which techniques and activities we select and which we reject.

Guiding principles

Modern English language teaching (**ELT**) is based on the culmination of years of second language learning research and practice, and is always developing. It does not offer a standard 'method' to follow in all classes or prescribe exactly what you should do but offers certain guiding principles which form an 'approach' to our teaching. The following important principles form the foundation for the ideas presented in this book.

We learn a language in order to communicate
The overall principle that has guided teaching methodology for many years now is that the purpose of learning a language is to communicate in that language. This means that the language you teach should be meaningful, natural, and useful to your learners.

We should respect the individuality of our learners
Learners learn in different ways, so that our role as teachers is to respond to their different needs and ensure that the way we teach and the activities and materials we use are appropriate for our learners' level, ability, and needs, and are varied enough to appeal to different styles of learning.

Learning should be a positive experience
Our job as teachers is to provide interesting, motivating, enjoyable, and engaging learning activities for our learners. Lessons need to have a clear aim, which the learners are aware of, so that there is a sense of purpose and cooperative atmosphere in the classroom.

We should enable our learners to reach their full potential
As well as making learning fun and appropriate for our learners, we need to help them achieve their personal best. This will involve a mixture of challenge and encouragement: working with them to set learning goals and encouraging them in their efforts. It will also involve helping them take responsibility for their own learning.

As you develop as a teacher you will elaborate and extend these principles and add more of your own, to form your own personal teaching philosophy.

The next stage

The next two units in this book will give examples of lessons that are based on these principles. Unit 2 covers language and has four sections: grammar, **functions**, vocabulary (**lexis**), and pronunciation. Section 3 covers skills and also has four sections: listening, reading, speaking, and writing.

Each section is introduced by a short description of the language area or skill being focused on. These are designed to give you a clearer idea of what you are teaching.

There are 'Comment' boxes at various points in the lessons, which are designed to highlight a teaching idea and make suggestions about how best to handle that particular point in the lesson.

The final unit gives some practical help with everyday teaching. It covers lesson and course planning, assessment, review, and remedial work and areas of classroom management such as classroom language and **error** correction techniques.

2 Focus on language

2.1 The structure of a language lesson

Introduction

Learners need to hear or read the language they are learning. This is sometimes called **input**.

A teacher's job is to provide this input, help learners understand it, and to give them practice in using it.

1 Input

A teacher should choose examples of the language that are appropriate for the learners. At any level it is important for the teacher to consider what language the learners may know already and what language is new.

2 Understanding

Learners need help to understand language that they have not met before. The teacher can provide an explanation, demonstrate the meaning with pictures or mime, or help learners to work out the meaning for themselves.

As well as understanding meaning, learners also need to understand how words, structures, and expressions are formed. They need to understand, for example, that adverbs like *slowly* are formed by adding *–ly* to the adjective and that other adverbs like *quickly* can also be formed in the same way. They need to understand, for example, that a structure like *If it rains tomorrow I'll stay at home* is formed by using the present tense in the 'If' half of the sentence and 'will' in the other half, and that they can use the same pattern to make other meanings, such as, *If it's sunny tomorrow, I'll go to the beach.* They need to understand, for example, that the expression *How about …?* is followed by the *–ing* form of the verb and they can use the same pattern to make many sentences, for example, *How about going for a walk?*

3 Practice

There is a step between understanding what something means and how it is formed, and being able to use it. This step is *practice*, and teachers need to give learners practice using new language so that they become confident and develop the ability to speak or write in a way that other people can understand. This means helping learners put sentences together, pronounce words and phrases correctly, use the right word or structure to fit the situation, and express themselves.

In the next section we will look in more detail at these three points and how to break them down into smaller steps. These steps are called the *stages* of a lesson.

The stages of a lesson

There are many ways to plan a lesson and in this section we are going to look at one example, a lesson on asking for directions. More examples of lessons will be given later on in the book, in Sample lessons 1–16, found in Unit 2 and Unit 3.

Before the lesson

Before the lesson it is important to consider what language the students know (**assumed knowledge**) and what will be new. In this example lesson, the teacher knows that the students have already been taught town places such as *library, museum, swimming pool, crossroads, traffic lights*, and so he will use this vocabulary in the lesson. He also knows that they have been taught *Where is …?* for example, *Where is the post office?* and that they can give simple answers like *Opposite the library*. He knows that they have been taught the present simple, for example *I go to school by bus*. He knows that they have been taught to make questions with *Do you …?* and *How …?*, for example, *Do you go to school by bus?* or *How do you go to school?* He will be able to use all of this language in the lesson without explaining it. It is only the new language that he will need to explain and practise. The new language is the **target language**: the focus of the lesson. In this lesson, the target language is the question, *How do you get to …?* and the answers, *Go straight on, turn left/right, take the … road on the left/right.*

Input

Lead-in

At the beginning of a lesson, it is important to get the learners' attention and stimulate their interest and curiosity. Beginning by asking students questions, instead of telling them things, is one good way. Encouraging students to predict what is going to come is another. For example, the teacher could begin a lesson on asking for directions by showing a picture of someone looking at a map in a city street and asking, *What's he doing? What's he going to do next?*

It is also important to set the scene for the reading or listening input. In this lesson, the teacher plans to use a short dialogue where someone asks for directions. But before this he needs to make sure that the learners understand the **context**: the situation, who the speakers are, and what the relationship is between them. In this lesson, the context is a lost tourist asking a stranger for directions. The teacher can use a picture to create the context, and ask the students, *Where do you think he wants to go?* so that they predict what he will say. This will help them understand the dialogue when they hear it.

Introduce target language

When the learners have understood the context, the teacher is ready to do a **presentation** of the target language. In this lesson, the target language is introduced in a listening task, which the teacher has on a cassette or CD (if this equipment is not available, he can act out the conversation):

TOURIST   *Excuse me. Can you help me?*
WOMAN   *Yes …*
TOURIST   *How do I get to the museum?*
WOMAN   *The museum … OK … Go straight on. Turn left at the lights.*
TOURIST   *Turn left at the traffic lights?*
WOMAN   *Yes, then take the first road on the right. The museum is opposite the library.*
TOURIST   *Thank you.*

It helps if the learners have a question or an **activity** to help them to focus their listening. The first time they listen, the teacher can use the same question as when he set the context (*Where does the tourist want to go?*), so that the students can check if they were right. The second time they listen, the teacher gives them a map marked with the museum and the place where the tourist and woman are standing. As they listen, they draw in the route or follow it with their fingers. Finally, the students are given the **transcript** (a written version of the listening **text**) so that they can follow the conversation as they listen.

Understanding

Checking comprehension

The teacher then gives the learners some questions about the conversation to check whether they have understood, for example, *Do you turn left or right at the traffic lights?* The learners listen and try to answer the questions. The teacher then draws the map on the board and asks a learner to draw in the route to the museum, while the other learners check that it is correct.

Language focus/focus on form

The teacher needs to make sure the learners know which language to focus on. In this case, they need to focus on *How do you get to …?* and the answers, *Go straight on, turn left/right, take the … road on the left/right.*

The teacher can explain the meaning of *How do I get to …?* using the picture of the tourist, saying *Where is the museum? He doesn't know. He can ask, 'Where is the museum?' or 'How do I get to the museum?'*

Learners may need more help with the meaning of the directions. The teacher can demonstrate these using simple blackboard diagrams.

The learners also need to understand how the structures are formed: they need to understand that *How do I get to …?* can be followed by *the + noun*, and that this pattern can be used to make different meanings. Clarifying this for learners is called **focus on form**. One way of highlighting form is in a **substitution table**.

How do I get to	the museum?
	the sports centre?
	the library?

Substitution tables can also be used for the directions:

Go	straight on			
Turn	left	at the	traffic lights	
	right		crossroads	
			roundabout	
Take	the	first	road on the	left
		second		right

Knowing the rule and understanding how a complete sentence is put together means that learners can then go on and create their own sentences.

Practice

Practise the language
At this point the learners need a chance to try the language out for themselves. This can be done in various ways. In this lesson the teacher begins with a **drill**, where the target language is repeated a number of times, to give the learners practice in pronouncing it. When the class repeats it together, it is a **choral drill**, and when the teacher changes an element of the sentence, as in the example below, it is a **substitution drill**.

TEACHER	*How do I get to the …?* [teacher shows a flashcard of library]
CLASS	*How do I get to the library?* [teacher shows a flashcard of swimming pool]
CLASS	*How do I get to the swimming pool?*

Then the teacher provides a **controlled practice** activity: this is an activity with a narrow language focus, meaning that the learners will need to use the new language when doing the activity. The controlled practice activity in this lesson is a role play. The teacher turns the classroom into a town centre, using the aisles between the desks as 'streets' and labelling desks with cards saying 'museum', 'library', etc. One learner comes to the front of the room and asks for directions, and the class gives them. The learner follows the directions, turning left and right down the 'streets'.

The learners then practise in pairs, using the map on the board with places labelled.

Notice how the students become more independent from the teacher as the practice activities progress. In the drill, the teacher directs what the students will say and how they say it. He can hear what the learners say and can give help and correct errors immediately. In the second activity, the learners have more choice about what to say, but the teacher can still hear everything they say and can help with errors and difficulties. In the third activity, the learners work in pairs and the teacher cannot hear what everyone is saying, though he can move round the classroom and listen to one pair at a time.

The teacher might decide that the learners would benefit from doing all three activities, the drill, the role play, and the pair work, or he might decide to go straight to the pair work from the drill. This will depend on how much help and support he thinks the students need from him before they are ready to work on their own.

There are many different activities for practising language: these are just three examples.

Feedback
During and after the practice stage the teacher also has a chance to provide feedback to learners. He can help them with their pronunciation and can correct errors. If the learners are really struggling, he can go back to an earlier stage and focus on the language again, explaining meaning and form, and then give more practice. In the whole-class activities, like the first two, he can hear everything the learners are saying and can help them directly. In the third activity he can listen in on the pairs and make a note of anything that the learners are struggling with or saying incorrectly. If many learners are struggling with the target language, the teacher may decide to stop the activity briefly and explain the language point again and check that the learners can produce it. If learners' errors are less important, the teacher can make a note of them and deal with them after the activity.

In general it is better to try to get learners to identify their errors and correct them themselves. The teacher can choose to do this in many ways, for example, by using finger correction. If the learners are saying *Turn right at crossroads* he can hold up five fingers and point to each finger in turn saying *Turn right at …* When he gets to the fourth finger he can pause and hold it, waiting for the learner to supply the right word. If the learner supplies *crossroads* the teacher can simply shake his head, point to the last finger, say *crossroads* and return to the fourth finger.

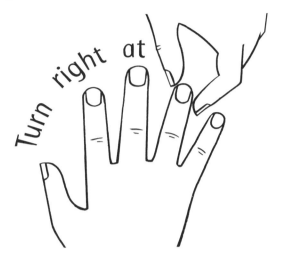

Another way of helping learners to correct their own errors is to write the incorrect sentence on the board and ask them what is wrong. This method should be used anonymously only, as you do not want to embarrass your students and stop them from contributing.

Use the new language
A final practice activity can give the learners a chance to see if they can use the target language to achieve a goal: this is known as **production**, or **free practice**. In this case the goal is to ask for directions, to give directions clearly, and to understand directions well enough to know where to go. Here is an example of an activity which challenges the learners to use the language in this way: the teacher divides the class into pairs: A and B. He gives A and B maps of the same town centre, but A has different places marked on his map from B:

A has to ask B for directions to the library, the museum, and the swimming pool. B has to ask A for directions to the sports centre, the park, and the art gallery. Each learner must follow the other's directions to mark the place on the map. This kind of activity, where learners have to get information from each other in order to complete the task, is called an **information gap activity**, and is very useful in language teaching, as it gives each learner a real need to communicate. To give this information, each learner will need to use the target language.

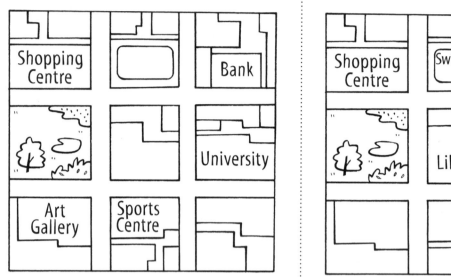
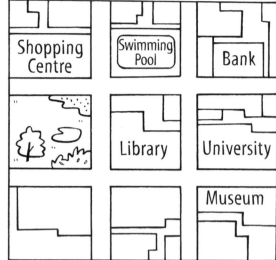

Consolidation

All the language in this lesson so far has been oral — speaking and listening. It can help learners to spend some time writing, either in the lesson or for homework. Writing is a slower, more reflective activity than speaking and gives learners more time to think about the language they need to express themselves. It also helps to fix the language in the learners' minds: this is called **consolidation**. A writing task to consolidate this target language could be: *Imagine you have invited someone to your house. Your friend has not come to your house before. Write a note or an email giving your friend directions to find your house.*

Different lesson structures

Teachers have a lot of choices when they plan their lessons. The above example is only one way of structuring a lesson.

It follows a model known as **Presentation-Practice-Production (PPP)**: during the presentation, the teacher presents (introduces) the target language, setting it in a real world context so that the learners can see how and when it is used. Often the teacher will finish a presentation with a focus on form. Then in the practice phase, the learners are given activities to focus on the target language, and finally, in the production phase, the learners are given speaking activities which give them the opportunity to use the target language in a more natural, realistic way.

In the **task-based learning (TBL)** model, the focus is on a **task** that the learners do while the teacher monitors their performance and assesses what language they need. Then the teacher introduces the language that the learners need, before giving them a task similar to the first one for them to practise it. The idea behind this model is that the first task will both encourage the learners to stretch their language to cope with new situations and will make them aware of their need for new language.

There is also the **test-teach-test** model, which has a similar order to TBL, as the lesson begins with an activity (test). The learners do this and then the teacher introduces the new language and practises it with them (teach). Finally, the learners do another task in pairs or groups (test). This model is similar to TBL in that the presentation stage comes after an activity or task, but differs in that in TBL, the language focus activity is based on whatever the learners need there and then: the language content is not decided in advance. In test-teach-test lessons, however, the teacher has decided in advance what new language he will introduce.

Individual lessons can vary from these three basic structures. Sometimes, for example, a teacher will need to introduce a lot of new language in one lesson, and may choose to divide it into two sets to present and practise separately before moving on to the production phase. Similarly, a grammar revision lesson could consist of a series of different practice activities. Even in a PPP lesson, if the learners are having difficulty at the production stage, the teacher may decide to present and practise the language again.

Whichever way a lesson is structured, it will be some combination of the stages we have looked at in this unit.

In sections 2.2–2.5 you will see examples of these different ways of structuring a lesson.

2.2 Focus on grammar

About grammar

Word order, word combinations, and word forms

Grammar is a description of the language system—it shows us how we order words in sentences, how we combine them and how we change the form of words to change their meaning.

In order to write the sentence:

He has a long holiday in July.

you would need to understand the system for ordering, combining, and changing words.

Word order
You would need to understand that the elements of a sentence come in a particular order:

Subject	Verb	Object	Adverbial phrase
He	has	a long holiday	in July

Individual words also come in a particular order:

The adjective *long* comes before the noun *holiday*, and the preposition *in* comes before the noun *July*.

Word combinations
Words can be combined with some words but not with others. You would need to know that we can say *a long holiday* not *a large holiday* or *a big holiday*. Similarly, we can say *in July* not *on July* or *at July*. This word-combining feature of language is called **collocation**.

Word forms
You would need to know that the verb *to have* changes to *has* with *he* or *she*. If you were asked to change the sentence to the past you would need to know that you change the word *has* to *had*.

If you have learnt English as a foreign language you will have learnt how to order, combine, and change words to make grammatically correct sentences. If English is your first language you will know instinctively how to do this, but you may not have explicit knowledge of the grammar system. There is not enough space to give a comprehensive introduction to grammar here, so you will need to do some further reading. Some grammar books are recommended in Further reading. But as a starting point, to help you approach a grammar book, here is a brief introduction to some ways of describing language.

Elements of a sentence

We can describe language in terms of elements of a sentence, for example:

Subject	Verb	Object
The dog	chased	the cat

The word order in a sentence in English is subject, verb, object: first: the **subject** (agent, or doer, of the action), second: the **verb** (the action), and third: the **object** (person or thing the action is done to). Other languages may have a different word order (for example, the word order in Japanese is subject, object, verb).

In a longer sentence there may be other sentence-elements, such as an adverbial phrase:

Subject	Verb	Object	Adverbial phrase
The dog	chased	the cat	up a tree

The adverbial phrase tells us a bit more about where, when, or how the action happened.

Some verbs, like *be* or *seem*, do not have an object. They have what is called a 'complement'.

The complement can tell us something about the subject:

Subject	Verb	Complement
I	am	happy

Parts of speech

Another good starting point is to know the names of the 'parts of speech'.

- **nouns**   car, moon, computer …
- **adjectives**   small, excited, old …
- **articles**   a, an, the
- **determiners**   some, many, this, that …
- **pronouns**   I, you, his, them …
- **verbs**   go, come, eat, speak …
- **adverbs**   quickly, slowly …
- **conjunctions**   and, but, although …
- **prepositions**   of, in, with, near, on …

A grammar book is usually organized into sections corresponding to these parts of speech. Each part of speech can be subdivided into different types. For example, under 'pronouns' you will find subject pronouns (*I, you, he, she, we, you, they*) and object pronouns (*me, you, him, her, us, you, them*). Different types of words will have a different set of conventions about how they can be used. For example, we can say: *The dog chased her* but not *The dog chased she*. There is a Grammar terminology appendix at the back of the book which gives a very basic introduction to some of the important categories of the parts of speech and what they are called. This guide to terminology should help you to approach a grammar book.

How to help learners with grammar

Teaching form

You will need to know grammatical terminology, but do you need to teach it to your students? In general it is best to avoid complicated grammatical terms, particularly with lower level students, though sometimes it is necessary. In general, it is easier for students to grasp a new structure if the language is presented visually, for example in a table, rather than analysed and described using grammatical terminology. A table makes it clear what the structure is and how it can be used to make other sentences:

Telling the students only: *The past continuous is made up of the past form of the verb BE with the present participle*, is far more difficult to understand. There is an example of visual presentation of grammar in Sample lesson 1 (page 23).

You do not always have to explain grammar rules to students. Often they can work them out for themselves, though you will probably need to give them some help by giving them a task, such as a chart to fill in or questions to answer to guide them towards 'discovering the rule'. There is an example of this in Sample lesson 2 (page 28).

Teaching meaning

So far we have looked at grammatical form — the correct ways of using word order and changing grammatical form. This is a vital part of grammar teaching but it is just as important to teach what structures mean and how they are used.

You should always introduce a new grammar structure in a meaningful context. This context should make the meaning of the new structure clear and show how it is used in real life. You will see in Sample lessons 1 and 2 how this is done, in these cases using drama and a reading text. The reading text in Sample lesson 2 is a questionnaire and it contains a number of examples of the new language which the learners can read in a context which will help them understand its meaning. In the drama context in Sample lesson 1, the teacher does not begin by presenting the learners with examples of the new language, but instead uses questions to try to get the learners to produce the target language themselves. This process is called **eliciting**. If the learners make mistakes, the teacher can take what they say and **recast** it (say it again but without the error) so that the students hear a correct version of the new language.

When you have created a context and introduced the target language you will have to check that your students understand how it is used, which you can do by asking **concept questions** (questions that focus on how the target language is used). There are examples of concept questions in Sample lesson 1. You may also have to clarify or give explanations of what a structure means and how it is used, which you can do verbally or visually. In Sample lesson 1 the teacher uses a diagram called a timeline to clarify meaning and to explain how the structure is used.

Practising and using the language

Practice activities help students to remember the new language and to become more accurate and more fluent in using it. There are many activities that you can use to practise the language. The practise and 'use the language' activities in the sample lessons in this book include questionnaires, written exercises, miming and matching games, drills, drama, and a written description.

In planning practice activities for your lesson, you need to have a balance between activities which improve **accuracy** (getting the grammatical form right) and **fluency** (communicating a message). Speaking activities such as drills, **gap fills**, or matching tasks, focus on accuracy. Others, such as information gap activities, discussion, and drama activities focus on fluency.

In writing activities, accuracy-focused activities include gap fill or matching exercises, and fluency-focused activities include short descriptions or stories. There are examples of these in Sample lessons 1 and 2.

It is important to vary the activities you use for presentation and practice activities — don't always begin with a reading text or always use drills for controlled practice. The number and type of activities you choose should be based on what kind of practice your learners need and how much practice you think they need. A weak class may need simpler practice activities or a greater number of practice activities, whereas a more confident class may be ready to move on to the production stage after a much shorter amount of practice.

2.2 Focus on grammar

How to select grammar items

Grammar items

In most cases you will be working with a book, or a school, or national **syllabus** where the grammar items are selected and ordered for you. In most syllabuses grammar items are carefully **graded,** meaning that simpler structures (for example, *This is my sister*) come before more complex ones (for example, *Not having seen him for five years, I was very surprised to bump into him again*).

However, learners often take time to process language they have been taught before they can start using it fluently and accurately, so you will need to **recycle** the grammar you have taught. You can choose items to teach or practise again:

- For revision
- For error correction and **remedial work**
- Because a grammar item is too big to be covered all at once: more complex items will need to be taught in small steps.

The structure of a grammar lesson

The two lessons that follow have a PPP structure (see Unit 2.1 page 16) but even when two lessons follow a similar order, there is room for a lot of variety in activities and techniques.

Sample lessons: focus on grammar

	Sample lesson 1	Sample lesson 2
Lesson structure	PPP	PPP
Language focus	Concept questions Timeline diagram	Students work out meaning themselves from context
Teaching focus	Eliciting language from students to guide them towards the target language	Encouraging students to work out the rule for themselves
Materials	Flashcards Jigsaw sentence slips	'Find someone who' slips Group questionnaire
Presenting the target language	Dramatized situation	Reading text with task
Practice activities	Drill Matching game Mime and guess game	Writing sentences about themselves Writing a questionnaire
Producing the target language	Drama activity Memory game	Using the questionnaires from the practice phase
Consolidation	Writing an account of a scene	Using a questionnaire the learners have written

2.2 Sample lesson 1

LEVEL	Pre-intermediate
LANGUAGE	Past continuous and past simple
	The past continuous gives the background to an event, for example:
	I was looking for my pet hamster, when X came in.
ASSUMED KNOWLEDGE	Present continuous, simple past
RESOURCES	Board, flashcards (Stages 2 and 6), handout slips with two halves of sentences (Stage 7)
PREPARATION	Draw the flashcards (Stages 2 and 6) and make the handout slips (Stage 7)
TIME GUIDE	45 minutes

Lead-in

1 Ask one student to leave the class. Tell him he will get a surprise when he gets back.

> **Comment**
> This creates a mystery which will engage the learners' attention.

2 Create the context: tell the rest of the class to imagine they are a (big) family. They have lost their pet hamster (use the flashcard in case this is a new word) and are looking for it everywhere. Get them to begin miming looking for the hamster. Then ask the student to come back in.

> **Comment**
> This is a fun way to introduce the language point that gets all the learners actively involved and provides a clear and dramatic context for an interrupted action. Other possible contexts could be: at a party when X arrives; doing housework when X comes round; watching a horror movie when the lights went out.

Introduce target language

3 Ask the student, *What were they doing when you came in?* Get him/her to guess. As he/she guesses, recast his/her language, for example:

S *They looked for something.*
T Yes ... *they were looking for something. What were they looking for? Can you guess?*

> **Comment**
> This way of introducing the language by asking questions is a very natural way of introducing language and keeps the learners more involved than if you simply tell them the new language.

2.2 Focus on grammar

Check comprehension

4 Start writing on the board the sentence: *We were looking for a hamster when X came in*, asking the class to give you the words to make up the sentence. As the words are given, write them up in the appropriate place until the class have constructed your sentence together.

> **Comment**
> This way of drawing out the information from your students is called eliciting. It is useful for seeing how much the students know collectively, and for keeping them involved in the presentation of new language.

Underline '*We were looking for a hamster*'. Ask the class, *Did this take a long time?* Underline '*X came in*'. Ask the same question. Write 'long' above '*We were looking for a hamster*' and 'short' above '*X came in*'.

> **Comment**
> This type of question is called a concept question. It checks that learners have understood the main idea behind the structure you are teaching, in this case that it is used to describe a long action interrupted by a shorter one.

You can illustrate the concept of how these verb tenses are used by drawing a timeline on the board: draw a long horizontal line on the board labelled 'PAST', 'NOW', and 'FUTURE'. Draw a wiggly line on top, starting at a point in the past and continuing towards 'NOW'. Now draw an arrow pointing down at the end of the wiggly line. Ask the class what the wiggly line shows ('We were looking': the long action) and what the arrow shows ('when X came in': the short action which interrupted it).

Ask the class what represents 'We were looking' (the long wiggly line), and what represents 'X came in' (the arrow).

> **Comment**
> Using a timeline on the board is a useful way of illustrating the concept behind many other verb tense combinations too. Look out for timelines in course books and other materials.

Language focus

5 Draw a substitution table on the board (you may need to remind your learners that the singular 'you' form is the same as the plural).

I He She	was			
		looking for the hamster	when	X came in
You We They	were			

> **Comment**
> A substitution table like this makes the pattern very clear to the learners. The highlights draw their attention to the word forms used.

Check comprehension 6 Show the class the first flashcard and ask them what the hamster was doing. Ask them what they think happened next. Show the second flashcard and ask them to make a sentence using '…–ing … when …' Repeat with the other pairs of cards.

Think about how the flashcards will be interpreted, and what sentences you are likely to be given.

> **Comment**
> This activity gives the learners a chance to consolidate their understanding of how the *was/were* …-*ing* … *when* … pattern is used and how to form more sentences using the pattern with new vocabulary. It develops the context from the introduction—and satisfies learners' curiosity!—showing how the 'story' finished.

Practise the language

7   Hand out the slips of paper. Each slip has one half of a sentence. Tell the class that they have to stand up and try to find the person with the other half of their sentence. If you think your learners will have trouble with the words, draw snake, bee, fly, spider on the board first. You can mime 'swallow' if they do not know it.

I was walking in the country	when I saw a snake
I was working in the garden	when I saw a lot of bees
I was drinking a cup of tea	when I swallowed a fly
I was having a shower	when I noticed a big spider

Comment
The answers to this activity are not fixed—the learners should have fun discussing which answers are possible and do not need to take it too seriously. It gives them a further opportunity to practise using the new language in a controlled way.

8   When the learners have found their 'other halves', ask them to sit together and prepare a mime of their sentence. Give them a few minutes to prepare. Put the learners in small groups and then tell the pairs to perform their mimes for the group. The rest of the group should guess what happened and make a sentence using, *was/were … –ing … when …*

Comment
This activity gives the learners an opportunity to use the language to create more new sentences. The activity is fairly controlled; learners can check if their sentences are correct themselves by looking at the slips of paper.

Use the language

9   Divide learners into two groups. Tell each group they were all in a street when a spaceship landed and two aliens got out. The people in the street should all be doing different things: shopping, drinking coffee, waiting for a bus, etc. Give them some time to prepare their scene for the other group. The other group should watch and try to notice what everyone is doing. Then get them to work in small groups to try to remember what everyone was doing.

1 Two people were waiting for a bus …
2 Yes and Pierre was eating … an ice-cream.

Circulate to listen to what they are saying. Make notes of any problems or errors and deal with these in feedback immediately after this activity.

Consolidation **10** Get learners to write an account of the scene they watched, for example, *It was a sunny Saturday afternoon and the street was full of people. Two girls were looking in a shop window …*, etc. They can continue the story in any way they like.

> **Comment**
> This activity gets the students to use the language more freely and to put it together with language they already know. They will use the language both in speaking—as they discuss what they remember about the scene—and in writing. Writing gives the students more time to think about the language and will help to consolidate what they have learnt.

2.2 Sample lesson 2

LEVEL   Lower intermediate

LANGUAGE   Superlative adjectives (*adjective + **est**; **most** + adjective*):

big	*biggest*
sad	*saddest*
young	*youngest*
old	*oldest*
early	*earliest*
easy	*easiest*
careful	*most careful*
boring	*most boring*
interesting	*most interesting*
difficult	*most difficult*

ASSUMED KNOWLEDGE   Comparative adjectives (for example, *bigger, sadder*, etc), present perfect for life experiences.

RESOURCES   'Find someone who' slips, group questionnaire

PREPARATION   Prepare the 'Find someone who' slips (see Stage 1) and the questionnaire (see Stage 2).

TIME GUIDE   40 minutes

Lead-in   **1**   Hand out slips of paper to half the class. Each slip has a 'Find someone who' instruction on it, using a comparative adjective, for the students to compare themselves with each other:

> Find someone who is taller than you and sit next to them.

> Find someone who has bigger feet than you and sit next to them.

> Find someone who has more careful handwriting than you and sit next to them.

Ask these students to get up and go round the class asking questions till they find the person and then sit next to them.

> **Comment**
> This activity starts the lesson in a lively and enjoyable way. It also reminds the learners what they know about comparatives, which will help them understand today's lesson on superlatives. A quick revision activity is a good way to start a lesson, particularly if it is done in an enjoyable format like this game.

Introduce target language

2 Put learners in groups of 6–8. Give each group a questionnaire. In your group, who:

• has the smallest feet	• has the biggest hands
• is the youngest	• has the most interesting hobby
• has the most careful handwriting	• takes the earliest train
• has the worst journey to class	• has the best idea for a party

Ask them to read the questionnaire and to work out the answers for their group. Go round while they are doing this, listening to them and helping with any problems.

Comment
Relating language to students' personal lives makes a motivating and interesting context. This questionnaire introduces the new language in written form. The students will know the adjectives *big*, *good* and their comparative forms *bigger*, *better* already so it should not be hard for them to work out the meaning of the new language for themselves.

Check comprehension

3 When they have finished, check they have understood by asking each group to give you one fact about their 'records'.

T *So, tell me one thing you found out.*
S *Angelika has the most brothers and sisters! Seven!*

Comment
This activity has two functions: it will show you whether students have understood well enough to begin to use the new language themselves. It also 'rounds off' the group work and brings the class back together as a whole, ready for the next activity.

Language focus

4 Put up the adjectives in the left-hand column (see LANGUAGE). Then ask what the difference is between the four groups of adjectives. If they need help, tell them to think of the number of **syllables** in each word.

5 Put the class into pairs. Write *biggest* at the top of the right-hand column. Ask the learners to fill in the rest of the column. Check the answers when they have finished.

> **Comment**
> Learners can fill in some words from the words in the questionnaire. They can try to work out the others themselves.

6 Tell the pairs to look at the first two groups again and decide how they could divide them into two more groups.

7 Ask pairs at random how they have divided the words and what reason they have. Ask them if they can think of a 'rule' for each group.

Group 1: One-syllable adjectives, e.g. *young* and *old*, add *–est*; *sad* and *big* end in **vowel** + **consonant** so the last consonant is doubled.

Group 2: Two-syllable adjectives ending in *y*, e.g. *happy* and *funny*, the *y* changes to *i* before *–est*.

Group 3: The majority of two-syllable adjectives (except those ending in *–y*) take *most* (for example, *most careful; most boring*) but some can have either form, (for example, *quieter/more quiet*).

Group 4: Adjectives with more than two syllables take *most* (for example, *most interesting; most difficult*)

8 Ask them to look at their questionnaire. Are there any adjectives that make a fifth group? Group 5: irregular adjectives: *good/best; bad/worst.*

> **Comment**
> Changing word endings to form the superlative is quite complicated. It involves a set of rules related to the number of syllables and the spelling of the adjectives. If they are given some examples and guided through the process by the teacher, the learners can work out the rules for themselves. Discovering grammar in this way, rather than being given information is a way of making learning more memorable.

Practise the language

9 Write up the following adjectives:

nice   bad   pretty   good   thin
beautiful   exciting   interesting   famous   happy

Get learners to work in pairs to discuss how to make the superlatives. Go through in class when they have finished: write up the words and ask learners to make a sentence about themselves using the words, for example: I *think Japanese food is the nicest.*

> **Comment**
> This activity gets learners to apply the rules they worked out in the previous activity and gives you the chance to check that they have understood correctly.

Use the language

10 Write on the board:

What is the best book you've ever read? Why?

Collect answers from different learners. Then get the learners to make five more questions in this pattern:

What is the _____ _____ you've ever _____? Why?

Go round to deal with problems and give help if needed.

> **Comment**
> This activity is fairly controlled. It focuses on accuracy: learners have time to think about the adjectives they are going to use and to get the form right. However there is also an element of creativity: learners can choose what questions they will write. This makes the activity more interesting.

11 When they are ready, put learners in pairs to ask and answer each other's questions. Circulate to listen to what the learners are saying, and to help if necessary. Make a note of errors so you can go through them later.

> **Comment**
> This activity gives the learners the opportunity to use the new language more freely. As they answer each other's questions, they will end up discussing their experiences. In this way the new language will be integrated with language they already have.

Consolidation

12 Ask the students to write a report on their partner's choices.

2.3 Focus on functions

About functions

A **ww** is the communicative purpose of a piece of language. For example, the purpose of this piece of language *Could you close the window, please?* is making a polite request. Here are some more examples:

Inviting	*Would you like to come round for supper?*
Suggesting	*Let's have a game of chess.*
Agreeing	*That's right!*
Giving opinions	*I think that's great.*
Greeting	*Hello!*

Functions are directly useful — if your learners can make a request using *Could I/you (+ infinitive)?* for example, they can ask for a train ticket, order a meal, ask someone for directions, ask a friend for help with a problem, and so on.

There are various ways of expressing a function. These variations are called **exponents**. For example, the function of requesting includes the following exponents:

Can you open the window?
Could you open the window, *please?*
Would you mind open*ing* the window?

Each exponent provides a frame for building new sentences. For example:

Could you	close	the door,	please?
	pass	the salt,	
	let	me know,	

One grammatical form can have several functions, for example, the modal verb *can* is used for the following functions:

Ability	I *can* swim.
Requests	*Can* you turn off the television, please?
Permission	*Can* I smoke here?
Possibility	It *can* be rainy at this time of year.

Functional language is often a fixed expression or 'chunk', for example:

Never mind.
It doesn't matter.
Of course.
Excuse me.

In these cases, the words in the chunk do not change and the learners can memorize the chunk in the same way as an item of vocabulary.

Social functions, such as inviting, requesting, etc., occur as an exchange between two (or more) people, for example:

A   *Would you like to come round for supper?*
B   *I'd love to.*

A   *Could you open this for me?*
B   *Yes, of course.*

It is important that learners can take part in both parts of the exchange, i.e. asking questions and answering. They can do this in class in pair work and role play activities. They need to be aware that the response is not always a straightforward *Yes* or *No*. For example, when we respond negatively to an invitation, we use, *I'd love to, but …* or, *I'm sorry, but …*, because a direct negative response might appear impolite.

The language we use depends on the situation and on the person we are talking to. We use different language to talk to a friend, a stranger, a waiter, a member of the family, and so on. We are more informal with people we know well and more formal with people we don't know. Look at this example, where the speaker is requesting that someone closes the door:

INFORMAL: Father to son   *Door!*
FORMAL: To a stranger   *Could you possibly close the door, please?*

Learners need to learn what language is appropriate in different situations and to have practice in choosing and using it.

How to help learners with functions

Introducing functions

Social functions occur naturally in conversation, so one of the best ways of introducing them is in a conversation. There are different ways of doing this. In the 'Asking for directions' lesson described in 2.1, the teacher used a taped dialogue. In Sample lesson 3 the teacher gets the learners to have a group discussion, then elicits from them what language they used for suggestions and builds on this by adding some new language for suggestions. In Sample lesson 4 the teacher has a real-life conversation with the learners, asking them to tidy up the classroom.

Functions and grammar

Because different exponents involve different grammatical forms, you have to be careful to show the learners clearly how the different forms are used to avoid confusion. Sample lesson 3 gives an example of this.

Functions and appropriacy

You can help clarify for your learners which exponents are more polite by presenting the different expressions with a 'cline' to show the degree of politeness (a list of exponents, with the most polite at the top), and by having a class discussion to match appropriate expressions to situations. Sample lesson 4 gives examples of both of these.

Practising functions

Learners need to practise both sides of social exchanges, so pair work, role play, and simulation are especially important practice activities. **Pair work** involves two learners practising both sides of a short exchange. **Role play** involves a pair or group imagining they are characters in a particular situation, for example, one friend inviting another to dinner, a customer complaining to a shop assistant, or a family giving opinions about which television programme to watch. A **simulation** is a role play where the whole classroom becomes an imaginary place, for example, a town centre where lost tourists ask inhabitants for directions, a row of shops where 'customers' buy things from 'assistants', or a restaurant where 'diners' order meals from 'waiters'. There are examples of all these activities in the lessons in this unit.

Written consolidation

Functional language can be written as well as spoken, though it can sometimes be more formal in writing. You can help to consolidate oral practice by getting learners to write realistic notes and letters. There are examples of how you can do this in Sample lessons 3 and 4.

Selecting functions

The functions you teach will need to be suitable for your learners' level and needs. A group of beginners planning a tourist visit to an English-speaking country will need functions such as *asking the way, asking for things in shops, ordering a meal*, and *booking a hotel room* expressed in very simple language. An advanced group of learners hoping to study in an English-speaking country will need functions necessary for academic study, such as *giving opinions, presenting an argument*, etc.

In a general English course, a cyclical approach is the best to use for teaching functions. This means that functions are taught more than once at different levels, using simpler language for the lower levels and gradually adding in more complex structures. So beginners might have a lesson on requests where they learnt *Can you …?*. At pre-intermediate they might add *Could you …?* and *Could you possibly …?* and by intermediate they might add *Would you mind ….–ing?*

The structure of a functions lesson

Sample lesson 4 is organized like the others we have looked at so far, following a PPP model, but Sample lesson 3 begins with a speaking activity before introducing the new language. This is because it is a test–teach–test lesson. The lesson begins with an activity which requires the new language (test). The learners complete this as best they can and then the teacher introduces the new language and practises it with them (teach). Finally the learners do another speaking task in pairs or groups (test). The idea behind this way of organizing a lesson is that the first speaking activity will encourage learners to stretch the language they have to cope with new situations, and that it will make them aware of their need for the new language.

Sample lessons: focus on functions

	Sample lesson 3	Sample lesson 4
Lesson structure	Test–teach–test	PPP
Language focus	Making and responding to suggestions	Making requests
Teaching focus	How to teach the different exponents of a function	How to teach appropriacy
Materials	Virtually no materials	Realia (classroom objects), flashcards, role cards
Presenting the target language	Teacher elicits language	Teacher uses classroom situation to introduce new language in context
Practice activities	Teacher–students question and answer 'Open pair' practice	Teacher–students discussion on appropriate language Whole class simulation
Producing the target language	Group discussion	Pair work Role play
Consolidation	Short notes and replies	Request letters and replies

2.3 Sample lesson 3

LEVEL	Lower intermediate
LANGUAGE	Making and reacting to suggestions:

How/What about going for a picnic?
Great!
Good idea.
Thanks, I'd love to.
That's a good idea, but …
Sounds good, but …
I'd like to, but …

ASSUMED KNOWLEDGE Vocabulary for leisure activities

Possibly some expressions for suggestions, for example, *Let's …/ Shall we …?*

RESOURCES Board, eight word/punctuation cards:

How about	going	to the beach	?
Let's	go	for a walk	.

PREPARATION Make the cards

TIME GUIDE 40 minutes

....

Lead-in **1** Tell the class that it's going to be warm and sunny at the weekend. Ask what sort of things they like doing outside at the weekend and put their suggestions in a list in the centre of the board. You can use a substitution table like this:

Outdoor activities

	for a	walk swim drive picnic
go	to the	beach park
	fishing cycling	

> **Comment**
> Asking learners about their personal preferences is a good way to introduce a topic and get the learners interested. It also provides the basis for the speaking activity in Stage 2.

Use the language

2 Put the learners into groups of three or four and ask them to talk about and decide what they are going to do at the weekend, using the ideas on the board. They should find a total of four activities to do together: one in the morning and one in the afternoon on each day. As the groups talk, walk round the class and write down the language they are using to make suggestions.

> **Comment**
> In this lesson the learners do a speaking activity before any new language is introduced. There are two main reasons for this:
>
> 1 It gives them an opportunity to use the language they already have. At this level learners may already be able to use some words and phrases to make suggestions. There needs to be a balance between teaching learners to use new language and giving them the chance to use the language that they already know.
>
> 2 It gives the teacher a chance to find out what language the learners can use. The teacher can use this information to make decisions about what language to introduce later on.

Language focus

3 When the groups have finished, ask them what they are going to do. Then ask them if they can remember any words or phrases they used to suggest something. Add any appropriate ideas to the board, on the left-hand side, for example, *Let's …/Shall we …?* etc.

Making suggestions		Outdoor activities	
Let's … Shall we …?	go	for a	walk swim drive picnic
		to the	beach park
		fishing cycling	

> **Comment**
> Stage 3 helps the learners to think about language they already know and can use. Talking about this as a class also allows the learners to learn from each other. Now you can go on to introduce new language.

Introduce the language

4 Put up a new speech bubble with *How about …?* and ask the class if they know how they should change the verb ending (Answer: add *–ing*). Do the same with *What about …?*

> **Comment**
> The most important feature of functional language is that we use it to do things with the language and to interact with other people. At the same time, we also need to make sure that the learners can put functional language together using the correct grammatical forms, for example, to use –ing endings or not.

Rub out the word *go* from the phrases on the board. Add *go* or *going* to the phrases for making suggestions on the board so that the learners can see how to make sentences.

Making suggestions	Outdoor activities	
		walk
	for a	swim
Let's **go** …		drive
Shall we **go** …?		picnic
	to the	beach
How about **going** …?		park
What about **going** …?	fishing	
	cycling	

Ask eight learners to come to the front, and give them each a word card. Get them to hold the card up so that the class can see it. Then ask them to sort themselves out into two sentences.

> **Comment**
> This 'human grammar' is a good visual way of demonstrating sentence structure to the learners.

5 Ask the class how we can respond to a suggestion and put up some examples on the board, for example:

Making suggestions	Outdoor activities		Responding		
Let's **go** … Shall we **go** …?	for a	walk swim drive picnic	YES		Great! Good idea! I'd love to!
How about **going** …? What about **going** …?	to the	beach	NO		Sounds good, but … That's a good idea, but … I'd like to, but …
	fishing cycling				

Ask the class why we don't just say *No* (Answer: this would not be polite).

> **Comment**
> You do not need to break these phrases down to teach the grammar: they can be learnt as set expressions or 'chunks' of language.

Check comprehension   **6** Make suggestions to individual learners and encourage them to respond using different expressions, for example:

TEACHER	*Kurt, how about going for a picnic?*
KURT	*Great! Where? The beach?*
TEACHER	*Sounds good.*
TEACHER	*Kyoko, how about going for a swim?*
KURT	*That's a good idea, but … the water is very cold.*

Practise the language   **7** Ask individual learners to make suggestions to other learners across the class, for example:

PIERRE	*Kyung Ae, how about going for a drive in my car with me?*
KYUNG AE	*I'd like to, but … er … I have to wash my hair.*

> **Comment**
> This kind of practice between two learners across the class, with the rest of the class listening, is a kind of pair work called open pair practice. It is a good way of giving realistic practice while allowing you to listen and correct mistakes or explain misunderstandings before freer practice. It makes a good basis for work later in groups or 'closed pairs', i.e. the whole class working in pairs.

Use the language   **8** Tell the class that you've just heard the weather forecast for the weekend and it has changed — it's going to rain on Sunday. Ask the class for some indoor ideas, and add them to your board, remembering that you have 'go' already in the 'Making suggestions' column. For example:

Making suggestions	Indoor activities		Responding
Let's **go** … Shall we **go** …?	to a restaurant to a concert to a museum	YES	Great! Good idea! I'd love to!
How about **going** …? What about **going** …?	to the cinema skating shopping	NO	Sounds good, but … That's a good idea, but … I'd like to, but …

Put the class back into their groups and get them to revise their plans for a rainy Sunday. Circulate to **monitor** their language and make a note of any problems and errors to feedback after the activity.

> **Comment**
> This lesson is based on the pattern:
> - first speaking activity
> - new language
> - second speaking activity.
>
> The second speaking activity is similar to the first but not exactly the same. This means that the learners can use similar language: the language they already know plus the new language. This means they can build on what they did in the first activity and improve their performance. You can build in interest and creativity by using a different context—a rainy day—and by putting the learners in different groups, so they are discussing different ideas with different people.

Consolidation

9 When the groups have finished, get each group to write four short notes to other groups, suggesting activities to do together. Collect up the notes and redistribute them at random. Students write replies according to whether they can come or not.

> We're going for a picnic on Saturday afternoon. How about coming too?

> Sorry! I'd love to but we're going cycling on Saturday.

2.3 Sample lesson 4

LEVEL Intermediate

LANGUAGE Making and responding to requests:

Could you …?
Of course or **Sorry, I'm afraid I can't …**

ASSUMED KNOWLEDGE *Can you …?* for requests

RESOURCES Board, role play cards, flashcards (see below)

PREPARATION

1 Make the flashcards above for stage 5. These should be big enough for the whole class to see.

2 Make these role play cards for each pair of students (see stage 7). If you have a large class and no copying facilities, you can put them on a large poster to stick on the board.

> You are going on holiday. Ask a friend to look after your cat.

> Dinner is nearly ready. Ask your son to set the table.

> Your car has broken down. Ask a neighbour to give you a lift.

> Tell your daughter to tidy her room.

> Ask a friend to lend you a good book

> You are going on holiday. Ask a neighbour to watch the house for you.

> It's raining. Ask a colleague to lend you an umbrella.

> You have a headache. Ask a colleague if they could give you an aspirin.

> Your sister is going to the shops. Ask if she could get you some stamps.

> You need change for the telephone. Ask a stranger to change a note.

TIME GUIDE 45 minutes

2.3 Focus on functions

Lead-in

1 Prepare the classroom so that some things are in the wrong place (for example, books, chairs, etc.), some windows are open, and the board has writing on. When the learners come in, ask them what is different about the room.

> **Comment**
> Asking the learners to identify what has changed will engage their attention as they look around and try and spot the differences

Introduce the language

2 Ask the learners to help you put things back. Use some language that they know already, for example, *Can you …?* Then add *Could you …?* and *Could you possibly …?*, being more polite for bigger requests. Small request: *Can you put the board rubber back, please?* But, big request: *Could you possibly pick up all those books?*

> **Comment**
> The new language is introduced in a very natural way in this context. If you begin with language the learners know already (*Can you …?*), then it is easy to understand that *Could you …?* is an alternative.

Language focus

3 Write up *Open the window* on the board. Ask the learners if this is polite. Ask if they know how to ask more politely. Write up suggestions in a cline, from impolite to polite, for example:

Open the window!   Not polite
Can you open the window?

           ↓   ↓

Could you open the window, please?
Could you possibly open the window, please?   Very polite

> **Comment**
> In Sample lesson 3 there was not much difference in meaning between the various ways of making suggestions. Here there is an important difference: the level of politeness. An expression that is appropriate in one situation will not be appropriate in another. An important part of this lesson—and of many lessons on functions—will be getting the learners to decide what language is appropriate in different situations.

Check comprehension

4 Give the learners some example situations:

Ask a friend to lend you a book.
Ask your teacher to lend you a book.
Ask a friend to lend you some money.
Ask your mother to lend you the car.

Discuss what they would say: in general, politeness depends on WHO you are speaking to and HOW BIG the request.

Practise the language

5 Tell the class *You are on a plane. Ask the flight attendant to get you some things.* Hold up the flashcards one at a time and ask what they are. Practise the pronunciation of the words. Hold up the first flashcard again and discuss how they could ask for it (*Could you get me a blanket?* or *Could you possibly get me a blanket?*). Practise pronunciation with them, showing how the words 'Could you' are run together to sound like /ˈkʊdʒə/.

> **Comment**
> This first practice activity focuses only on the language that is new in this lesson and gives a context for making polite requests. You need to decide how accurately your learners need to speak. If you insist on only very accurate pronunciation, they may lose motivation. However, if their pronunciation isn't clear, other people might not be able to understand.

Repeat with the other flashcards getting the class to ask you to get things. Reply as if you are the flight attendant, choosing *Of course,* for some requests, and *I'm sorry I'm afraid I can't — we haven't got any left,* for others (for example, headphones, meal, etc.). Put up some example replies.

Of course!
Sorry, I'm afraid I can't.

6 Now get students to arrange the classroom like a plane with rows of seats and aisles between them. (In a traditional classroom layout this will not involve rearrangement.) Tell the class to imagine they are on a plane and they need the flight attendant to get them something. Ask five or six learners to be flight attendants and to walk down the aisles answering passengers' requests.

> **Comment**
> This kind of role play where the classroom becomes a place like an aeroplane, a restaurant or a shopping centre is called a simulation. It is a good way of creating a realistic context for practising 'situational' language like ordering meals, buying food, or, in this case, in-flight requests.

Use the language

7 Now put learners in pairs. Give each pair a set of role play cards (or use the poster you have made). Ask them to put them face down on the desk and to turn up one at a time. They should take it in turns to make the request and to reply.

2.3 Focus on functions

Feedback

8 Go through the situations with the class, discussing what would be the appropriate language for each situation.

Consolidation

9 Ask learners to imagine they cannot come to class. Ask them to write two short notes, one to a friend and one to a teacher, asking them to do something (for example, give in homework, collect worksheets, etc.). Collect these in and give them out again to different learners. Ask them to write a short reply.

2.4 Focus on vocabulary

About vocabulary

A vocabulary item, sometimes called a **lexical item**, can be:

- a single word, for example, *cat*, *table*
- two or three words that go together to make one meaning, for example, a noun like *washing machine* or a **phrasal verb** like *pass out* or *come up with*
- a multi-word phrase or chunk of language like *as a matter of fact*, *never mind*, *by the way*.

In each language learner's mind there is **productive vocabulary**: words that they are able to produce, themselves, for example, *shoes*, and there is **receptive vocabulary**: words that they understand but may never produce, for example, *afflict*. We all have a much bigger receptive vocabulary than a productive vocabulary.

Learners need to know:

- how a word is spelt
- how it is pronounced
- the meaning of the word
- what part of speech it is
- which words it is often used with (collocation)
- how the word is used: in what situations and contexts.

Spelling and pronunciation

Spelling and pronunciation are not easy because there is no consistent one-to-one relationship between a sound and how it is spelt. For example, /ɑɪ/ can be spelt with an 'i' as in *mind* or a 'y' as in *my*. Learners need help understanding the various ways sounds can be represented. One way of doing this is to group words which have the same sounds and same spelling, for example:

/ɑɪ/ bicycle, climb, nine, five, white
try, my, cry,
high, flight

Meaning

Some words refer to concrete things or actions, for example, *bus*, or *jump*. Other words refer to abstract concepts, for example, *beauty*, *existence*, *admire*.

It is important to teach words in context, because many words have different meanings when used in different situations, for example, *admit* can mean two very different things according to context: *He will admit to causing the accident* = confess; *This ticket will admit you to the concert* = allow you to go.

Words can have a literal meaning or a figurative meaning. In *We climbed a mountain*, the word 'mountain' refers to an actual mountain, but in *I've got a mountain of work to get through*, the word 'mountain' is used as an image of a huge pile of work. An **idiom** is a group of words which has a meaning different from the meaning of the individual words: for example, the question *Would you like a piece of cake?* refers to an actual slice of cake but the idiom *It was a piece of cake* simply means 'It was very easy'. **Idiomatic language** is common in conversational English.

We can often change the meanings of words by adding **affixes**. An affix is a group of letters added to a word, either at the beginning of the word (**prefixes**) or at the end of the word (**suffixes**) to change the meaning in some way. For example: the adjective *selfish* can be changed into its opposite by adding the prefix *un–*, or into a noun by adding the suffix *–ness*, or into an adverb by adding the suffix *–ly*: *unselfish; selfishness; selfishly*. It is important to teach which prefixes and suffixes can be used, for example, the negative prefix for *kind* is *un–*: *unkind*; but the negative prefix for *formal* is *in–*: *informal*. The noun suffix for the verb *collect* is *–ion*: *collection*, but for the verb disappear is *–ance*: *disappearance*.

Parts of speech

Every word belongs to a category or part of speech, for example, a verb, an adjective, a noun, an adverb. Each category has grammar rules associated with it, for example, all adjectives come before a noun in a noun phrase as in *a beautiful day* and adverbs usually follow the verb they are describing as in *The examination went well*.

When we add a suffix we change the part of speech that the word belongs to and this will change how the word can be used, for example we could say, *she had a happy smile*, but *she smiled happily*.

Collocation

Words are used together, in partnerships. This relationship between words is called collocation. For example, verbs collocating with *a party* include *have, go to, gatecrash,* and *throw* but not *make* or *do*.

Lexical sets and word fields

Vocabulary (**lexis**) is often taught in lexical sets or word fields. These are groups of words related by topic. A **lexical set** is a group of the same category of words, so for example, *table, chair, sofa,* and *bed* are all nouns belonging to the lexical set *furniture*; and *angry, happy, sad,* and *anxious* are all adjectives belonging to the lexical set *emotions*. A **word field** is wider than a lexical set and contains words and phrases loosely connected to a topic, so for example, the word field *relationships* might include the lexical set *family members* (*mother, father, sister,* etc.) but also other words and phrases like *friendship, close, distant, marriage, divorce, to be in love with, to break up with,* etc.

Register and appropriacy

Different words and phrases are used by different people, according to the situation and the relationship between the speakers. For example, the two phrases, *The concert was very enjoyable* and *The gig was awesome!* both have a similar meaning but *gig* and *awesome* are more likely to be used by younger people, while *concert* and *very enjoyable* are more likely to be used by older people. *Gig* and *awesome* are informal: they have a lower register than *concert* and *very enjoyable*. The term **register** is used to describe these differences in formality, and we talk about register as going from high'(formal language) to low (informal). Within lower register language is **colloquial** language, which is language used in conversation. Knowing which register to use in a situation is having an awareness of **appropriacy**. For example, ending an email to a work colleague with *Best wishes* would be appropriate because this is a formal ending, but to a close friend it would be inappropriate, as it is too polite.

How to help learners with vocabulary

Introducing and explaining vocabulary

Vocabulary can be presented in dialogues and reading passages where the new words appear in context and in combination with other words. You can also use pictures, mime, and **realia** (real objects) to introduce and explain the meanings of simple concrete nouns like *apple* or verbs like *swim*. With more abstract words you can explain meaning with:

- a definition: *poverty means you have very little money*
- an example: *furniture: beds, tables, and chairs are all furniture*
- a **synonym**: *spiteful means cruel, unkind*
- an **antonym**: *spiteful is the opposite of kind*
- related words: *tinkle and clatter are both noises. Tinkle is high, clatter is low: imagine you are washing up — the pans clatter, the glasses tinkle.*
- translation: sometimes this is the quickest way to explain, but be careful — the translation might not be the exact meaning of the new word.

Helping learners record new words

Learners need to develop study skills such as:

Recording new words

It will help learners if they can record their new words in a vocabulary notebook or on small cards. Vocabulary notebooks can have pages divided down the centre with new words on one side and meanings on the other. Small cards can have the word on one side and the meaning on the other. Learners can record the meaning as a translation, or with a definition in English. Whichever way they choose, it is helpful if they record their new words in phrases or sentences that show how they are used.

Organizing new words in lexical sets or word fields

It will help learners if their words are recorded in groups of words related by topic. Two ways of doing this are demonstrated in Sample lessons 5 and 6, which use mind maps and labelled pictures.

Helping learners remember new words

Simply recording words is not enough—learners need to spend time memorizing new vocabulary. They can do this by themselves out of class, but you can also give them help with memorization, through repetition and personalization. Repetition is effective—but it can be boring! You can help make it fun by turning it into a game, as in Sample lesson 5, which uses a memory game. Personalization involves the learners giving the new words some sort of personal association. Sample lesson 6 shows a 'personalizing' activity.

Helping learners use new words

Once learners have had time to absorb the new vocabulary they can begin to use it communicatively. Words cannot be used in isolation: they have to be used in combination with other language. Sample lessons 5 and 6 show how new vocabulary can be integrated with language the learners already know to help them communicate.

Recycling vocabulary

Remembering words is a long process; even if learners can remember and use new words by the end of a lesson, they may have forgotten them a week later. You will need to revise and recycle the new vocabulary to make sure they retain it.

How to select vocabulary

Frequency

Some words are used more frequently than others, for example, words such as *eat* and *school* are used more often than words such as *distract* or *security*. It makes sense to teach the more frequent words earlier in a syllabus at lower levels. Most monolingual learners' dictionaries will give an indication of frequency.

Word fields

Learning words that are grouped around a topic is easier and more meaningful for learners than learning lists of unconnected words, and gives learners a good basis for a conversation or discussion on that topic. Most teaching materials combine frequency and topic as a basis for choosing what vocabulary to teach.

The structure of a vocabulary lesson

Lesson 5 focuses on concrete vocabulary that can be introduced in a direct way using physical objects, and this type of lexical set is easily taught using the PPP structure that we have seen before. In Lesson 6, however, the vocabulary is abstract and needs to be explained with simple definitions and examples. For this reason, some of the vocabulary is introduced at the beginning, and more is introduced later in the lesson, after some practice: the lesson uses two cycles of PPP to make it easier for the learners to handle so much new vocabulary.

Sample lessons: focus on vocabulary

	Sample lesson 5	Sample lesson 6
Lesson structure	PPP	PPP (x 2)
Language focus	Concrete vocabulary: crockery and cutlery	Abstract vocabulary: adjectives for describing character
Teaching focus	How to teach a lexical set of concrete nouns	How to teach a lexical set of abstract adjectives
Materials	Realia Poster	Flashcards Word cards, photos, magazine pictures
Presenting the target language	Introduced and explained using physical objects	Explained with simple definitions and examples
Recording the target language	Labelling a picture	Making a mind map
Practice activities	Whole class memory games	Pair work discussion: describing photos
Producing the target language	Information gap: spot the difference	Pair work discussion
Consolidation	Write a description	Write a 'Lonely hearts' advertisement

2.4 Sample lesson 5

LEVEL	Elementary
LANGUAGE	Crockery and cutlery:

knife   **fork**
spoon   **plate**
cup   **bowl**
saucer **glass**

ASSUMED KNOWLEDGE	*There is/there are*

House and furniture, for example, *table, chair, cupboard, sink, fridge, floor*

Prepositions of place: *in, on, next to, on the left/right*

RESOURCES   A selection of crockery and cutlery as above; table or desk, tablemat, tablecloth, tray, apron; poster of a kitchen

PREPARATION   Collect the items together (see Stages 2–3), and make the poster, or be prepared to do blackboard drawings (see Stage 9). If you have copying facilities, you can copy the poster as a picture, one for each student.

TIME GUIDE   40 minutes

Lead-in

1 Arrange a table and two chairs at the front of the class and put the tablecloth and mat on it. Write the name of a restaurant on the board, for example, The Pizza Palace. Ask the class *Where are we?* Ask a volunteer student to come to the front and put on the apron. Ask *Who is she/he?* Teach *waiter/waitress* if the learners do not know it. Tell them this is a new waiter/waitress and that it's their first day at work.

> **Comment**
> Creating a context for introducing the new words will make a livelier lesson than if you simply held the items up and said the words. Another context could be: teaching a child to set the table, or asking someone to pass you items.

Introduce the language

2 Tell the class you are the restaurant boss. You are going to teach the new waiter to set the restaurant table. Hand them a plate, saying, *Put the plate on the mat.* Continue handing over items and telling the 'waiter' where to put them, for example, *Put the knife on the right. Put the bowl on the plate*, etc. If they don't understand at first, show them with gestures.

> **Comment**
> Using real objects (realia) and actions makes the lesson more interesting and helps to make the new language memorable.

Language focus

3 Hold the items up and get the learners to repeat the words to practise pronunciation. Write the words in a list on one side of the board. When you write knife, show the learners that the 'k' is not pronounced by covering it up as you repeat the word.

4 Put up a simple picture of the table setting on the board.

2.4 Focus on vocabulary

Get the learners to copy the picture in their vocabulary books. Ask them to label the picture with the words from the list on the board.

> **Comment**
> It is important to get learners to record and store the new words. Recording new words in a vocabulary notebook is a useful habit. It will help them if
> 1 they can record words in lexical sets or under topics (here crockery and cutlery)
> 2 they can develop visual, kinaesthetic, or tactile associations with the words (here: through real objects, mime, and pictures).

Check comprehension 5 Get learners to check in pairs how they have labelled their pictures. Then get individual learners to come to the board and label the drawing.

Practise the language 6 Ask learners to close their eyes. Erase one item (and label) from the picture on the board. Get learners to open their eyes and tell you what is missing. Get learners to take turns in coming up and erasing an item for the class to identify.

> **Comment**
> Repetition will help memorization. However, repetition can easily become boring and meaningless. This game and the two that follow help to make repetition both meaningful and fun.

7 Put a number of items on the tray, for example, two cups, four knives, one spoon, etc. Tell the students they can look at the tray for 30 seconds. Then put the cloth over the tray. Put learners in pairs to say what they remember, for example,

ABDUL *Three cups!*
KEIKO *No, there are two cups.*

Ask learners what they remember. Write on the board as they tell you:

There is	one	spoon
There are	two	cups
	four	knives
There aren't	any	bowls

Encourage learners to tell you in complete sentences. Then take the cloth off the tray. Get learners to say whether the sentences were right or wrong. Draw attention to the plural of knife, by highlighting it: kni<mark>ve</mark>s.

Use the language

8 Put the poster on the board and get learners to copy it onto a piece of paper (or hand out copies to each student). Tell the learners that this is a kitchen after a party, and so it's messy. Get the learners to draw in crockery and cutlery items in different places in the room. Show them how to do this by drawing in a couple of examples on the poster. They can put the items anywhere they like. When they have finished, put them in pairs. Tell them not to show their pictures to each other; they should find the differences between their pictures. Put up speech bubbles as an example of what to say.

> In my picture there is a spoon on the table.

> In my picture there aren't any spoons – but there are two knives.

Go round listening to your learners as they do this and when they have finished, give feedback, putting up errors on the board and asking the class to correct them.

Consolidation

9 Ask learners to write a description of their picture. Collect in the descriptions and the pictures. Pin the pictures up round the room. Hand out the descriptions to the learners so each gets a new description. They should go round the room and try and find the picture that matches their description.

2.4 Sample lesson 6

LEVEL	Intermediate
LANGUAGE	Adjectives for describing character

energetic	**efficient**	**practical**
laid back	**disorganized**	**dreamy**
selfish	**sociable**	**funny**
unselfish	**shy**	**serious**

ASSUMED KNOWLEDGE	Some simple adjectives for character, for example, *nice, tidy, kind*, etc.
RESOURCES	Board, flashcards, magazine pictures of men and women, word cards of the new adjectives
PREPARATION	Make the flashcards (see Stage 1) and word cards (see Stage 3). Ask the class to bring photos of their family (see Stage 7). Collect magazine pictures of men and women, one for each pair (see Stage 10).
TIME GUIDE	40 minutes

Lead-in   **1**   Show the class the flashcards of your family (these could be photos of your family, or pictures from a magazine). Ask them who they think the people are: your sister, your father, etc. Tell them the names, for example, *Anne, John, Mary, Tony*, and write them up on the board.

Introduce the language   **2**   Put up the four flashcards. Tell them you are going to talk a bit about your family. They should listen and match names and pictures.

Talk about your family, for example,

My brother John is the eldest. He's very energetic and efficient: he's a doctor, so he works long hours, but he has a lot of hobbies and is very busy all the time. He's very practical and good with his hands … he's very different from my other brother. Tony's laid back and relaxed, loves films, books, theatre. He's very disorganized and untidy — a bit dreamy — not good with money! My sisters are very different too. Anne's very sociable, she loves people and parties. She's very funny — makes everyone laugh. She's got a strong personality — can be a bit selfish. Mary is just the opposite: she's very shy, quiet and serious, but she's a really nice person, kind and unselfish.

> **Comment**
> This vocabulary is abstract and cannot be explained as easily as the vocabulary in Sample lesson 5. However, using a picture to give a general idea is a good starting point. As you talk, you can give examples which will help learners to understand the meaning of the new words, for example, *Anne is sociable—she loves people and parties.*

Check comprehension

3 Check whether the learners have matched flashcards and names correctly. Write the correct names under the flashcards. Give out the word cards to students around the class and tell them you'll repeat the description. They should come and put the card on the board under the right picture.

> **Comment**
> Matching words and pictures is a very useful exercise in vocabulary teaching: it encourages learners to guess the meaning of new words and helps you to check comprehension and explain words as you go through the answers.

Language focus

4 Ask learners to look at the lists of words under John and Tony and to match the opposites. Go through it with them. If learners do not know a word, explain in a simple way, for example, *efficient means you can do everything well and quickly.* Repeat with the words under Mary and Anne.

> **Comment**
> You cannot show the meaning of abstract words with pictures or realia. You will have to develop the skill of explaining simply. This means:
> - using simple words
> - using simple structures
> - using examples.

5   Get the class to practise saying the words. Make sure that they can say the words using the correct **stress**, i.e.

ener**get**ic   e**ffi**cient

6   Get learners to record the words in their vocabulary books. A **mind map** is a good way to record vocabulary. You can turn your board into a mind map so that they can copy it or you can get learners to make their own. If this seems too hard, you can give them part of the mind map, and get them to complete it.

energetic / laid back
(busy, works hard) (relaxed)

efficient / disorganized
(does everthing well (untidy, inefficient)
and quickly)

funny / serious
(makes people laugh) (sensible,
thoughtful,
careful)

Personality

practical / dreamy
(sensible and realistic) (has a lot of
imagination and
is not realistic)

selfish / unselfish
(thinks of self first) (kind, generous, thinks
of other people)

shy / sociable
(nervous of meeting (likes meeting and
speaking to people) speaking to people)

> **Comment**
> When learners create a mind map of vocabulary they need to think how to organize the words into categories This means they are processing the vocabulary—not just writing down the words but thinking about them which will help them to remember the words.

Practise the language

7   Ask students to look at their family photos and to think how they would describe their family members. Circulate as they do this and supply any more adjectives they need. Put students in pairs and ask them to describe their family photos to each other.

> **Comment**
> The pair work activity asks them to personalize the new words by relating them to their own lives. Personalization will create associations which help them memorize. The activity is in two stages. Learners need time to process new information before they can use it. This activity gives them time to recall new words and plan out how they can use them before they talk to their partner.

Language focus

8   When they have finished, ask learners to provide any more words they thought of. Add these to the mind map on the board, explaining the meaning for other learners if necessary. Ask for any more words they need and add these.

> **Comment**
> With beginners, you can be sure what vocabulary they know and what is new. With intermediate learners you are less sure: they come from different backgrounds and will know different vocabulary. An activity like this draws on the combined knowledge of the class to increase vocabulary.

Practise the language

9   Put learners in new pairs and get them to describe their family to their new partner. Circulate, to monitor and help if necessary.

> **Comment**
> Repeating an activity with some extra language input and a new partner can be very motivating for learners: it means they have extra time to think and have a chance to 'improve on' their first effort.

Use the language

10   Give out the magazine pictures of men and women, one per pair. Get the learners to discuss their picture—*What is he/she like?*

Consolidation

11   Put up a framework for a Lonely Hearts advert:

_____, _____ , _____ man/woman,
aged _____, interested in _____ and _____,
would like to meet _____, _____ man/woman with
similar interests.

Ask the pairs to write an advert for their picture. They should use the adjectives on the board to help them complete the framework. Give an example: *Young, energetic, sociable man, aged 26, interested in art and cinema, would like to meet intelligent, attractive woman with similar interests.* Collect in the adverts and pin them round the room. Get learners to go round in pairs to see if they can find a suitable match for their character. If this activity is not culturally appropriate for your learners, simply get them to write a description of their picture. Then number the pictures and pin them up round the room. Collect in the descriptions and give them out at random. Learners go round the room to find the picture they think matches their description.

2.5 Focus on pronunciation

About pronunciation

There are many different varieties of spoken English in the world, but all spoken English has the following features:

- individual sounds
- word stress
- sentence stress
- connected speech
- intonation

Individual sounds

English has 44 different sounds, or **phonemes**. These can be written in a special alphabet called **phonetic script**:

The phonemes of English

Consonant sounds					
p	pen	/pen/	s	see	/siː/
b	bad	/bæd/	z	zoo	/zuː/
t	tea	/tiː/	ʃ	shoe	/ʃuː/
d	did	/dɪd/	v	vision	/ˈvɪʒn/
k	cat	/kæt/	h	hat	/hæt/
g	get	/get/	m	man	/mæn/
tʃ	chain	/tʃeɪn/	n	now	/naʊ/
dʒ	jam	/dʒæm/	s	sing	/sɪŋ/
f	fall	/fɔːl/	l	leg	/leg/
v	van	/væn/	r	red	/red/
θ	thin	/θɪn/	j	yes	/jes/
ð	this	/ðɪs/	w	wet	/wet/

Vowel sounds					
iː	see	/siː/	eɪ	say	/seɪ/
ɪ	sit	/sɪt/	əʊ	go	/gəʊ/
e	ten	/ten/	aɪ	my	/maɪ/
æ	cat	/kæt/	ɔɪ	boy	/bɔɪ/
ɑ	father	/ˈfɑːðə/	aʊ	now	/naʊ/
ɒ	got	/gɒt/	ɪə	near	/nɪə/
ɔ	saw	/sɔː/	eə	hair	/heə/
ʊ	put	/pʊt/	ʊə	pure	/pʊə/
uː	too	/tuː/			
ʌ	cup	/kʌp/			
ɜː	fur	/fɜː/			
ə	about	/əˈbaʊt/			

Learners need to be able to distinguish the difference between sounds which are similar, for example, the sounds /p/ and /b/ in words like *pin* and *bin*, the /ɪ/ and /iː/ sounds in *ship* and *sheep*. A pair of words like this with one difference in sound is called a **minimal pair**. In Sample lesson 8 you can see an example of how to use minimal pairs to help learners distinguish sounds they find hard to tell apart.

The phoneme table is adapted from the *Oxford Advanced Learner's Dictionary, Seventh Edition.*

Word stress

Words are made up of one or more sound units or syllables, a combination of vowels and consonants. For example:

Number of syllables	Example word
one	bus
two	to-night
three	ex-pen-sive
four	in-vi-ta-tion

With words of two syllables or more, one syllable is stressed more than the others:

to**night**   ex**pen**sive   inv**it**ation

Learners need to be able to both recognize and produce these stress patterns.

Sentence stress

Stress patterns also extend over a sentence. These are often the words that refer to new information. For example:

When are you **go**ing to see **John**?
I'll **prob**ably see him on **Mon**day.

A sentence may be said in different ways depending on what the speaker wants to emphasize. In the example below, *I'm seeing John on Monday*, the sentence stress changes to emphasize the most important information:

Are you seeing John on Tuesday?
No, I'm seeing John on **Mon**day

Are you seeing Sue on Monday?
No, I'm seeing **John** on Monday

Connected speech

Words often flow into each other especially when one word ends with a consonant sound and the next word begins with a vowel sound, for example, the /n/ and /ɑː/ in *When are you …?*, or the /l/ and /ɒ/ in *whole of*, where the letter 'e' in *whole* is not pronounced.

Similarly, in *four hours* the letter 'h' is not pronounced so the /r/ links with /aʊ/. These are all examples of linking. Another example of linking is when two consonant sounds come together and one consonant sound is lost, as in *next twenty*, which is pronounced /neksˈtwenti/ (*nextwenty*). When two vowels come together, a /w/ or /j/ sound is pronounced to link them together: *too old* becomes /tuːˈwəʊld/ (*too-w-old*); *see into* becomes /siːˈjɪntuː/ *see-y-into*. Try saying these words slowly to practise the linking.

Two other features of connected speech are contractions and weak forms. A **contraction** is when a full form such as *I am* is shortened to *I'm*. A **weak form** is when a vowel sound like the /æ/ in *have* is not stressed, as in the sentence ***How** many **sis**ters have you **got**?* Because the stress is on other syllables, the vowel of *have* becomes the weak sound /ə/. This weak vowel is called **schwa** and is the most common sound in English.

Intonation

The pitch of a speaker's voice can go up or down at the end of a sentence—this is called **intonation**. The patterns and rules about intonation are complex, but there are some simple patterns that we can recognize, for example:

Have you finished work yet?   *Not yet.*

How to help learners with pronunciation

An understanding of the features of pronunciation helps learners understand when they listen to the language. It also helps them to produce the language more accurately, though learners do not necessarily need to pronounce English perfectly, just well enough for other people to understand them.

Stress and intonation

You can help learners recognize stress by getting them to listen and mark in stressed syllables in a text as you read. They can learn to recognize intonation in a similar way by marking arrows on a text to show rising or falling intonation. Kinaesthetic activities are good ways of learning to recognize stress and intonation: learners can tap, clap, or walk out the rhythm of a text, or use hand gestures to show intonation. Drama activities such as rehearsing and acting out dialogues are also good for highlighting stress and intonation, as are **jazz chants**. There are examples of all these techniques in Sample lessons 7 and 8.

Connected speech

Dictations and gap fill texts are good ways of helping learners to recognize how words are connected in speech. Alternatively you can play or read them a short segment of text and ask them simply to count how many words or give them the text, ask them to listen and read at the same time and mark in which words are connected. There are examples of these activities in Sample lessons 7 and 8.

How to select pronunciation points

Pronunciation is best integrated with other language teaching points, not taught in isolation. In Sample lesson 7, for example, learners listen to some adverts and then work in groups to write and perform a television advert of their own. In between they practise the pronunciation of linked words and intonation in questions, which will help them when they come to perform their television adverts. In Sample lesson 8, learners use the adjectives in an activity before and after a focus on word stress.

The structure of a pronunciation lesson

These two lessons use lesson structures we have met before. Lesson 7 uses two cycles of PPP: first linking is introduced and practised, then intonation is introduced and practised, and then both are practised together. Lesson 8 has a Test-teach-test structure, beginning with a pair work speaking activity, then introducing and practising new language, and finally repeating the speaking activity with a change of partner.

Sample lessons: focus on pronunciation

	Sample lesson 7	Sample lesson 8
Lesson structure	PPP	Test–teach–test
Language focus	Linking Intonation	Sounds (*schwa*) Stress in *wh–* questions and statements
Teaching focus	Using voice and gesture to highlight features of pronunciation	Using gesture and actions to highlight features of pronunciation
Materials	Flashcards Poster Realia	Poster of jazz chant Flashcards
Presenting the target language	Reading a text aloud for students to hear the word linking and intonation	Eliciting unstressed syllables
Practice activities	Counting words Gap fill dictation Gestures	Identifying syllables Identifying stress Identifying *schwa* Clapping rhythm
Producing the target language	Guided writing	Writing a role play
Consolidation	Group writing and performance	Performing the role play

2.5 Sample lesson 7

LEVEL	Intermediate
LANGUAGE	Word linking:
	You'll be amazed.
	Intonation in questions and statements
ASSUMED KNOWLEDGE	Present simple, yes/no questions, imperatives, will
RESOURCES	Flashcards:

Realia: a floor cleaner, pet food, face cream, powdered food sachet, and other household products, one per 3–4 students
Poster with text of advert

PREPARATION — Prepare flashcards and realia. Re-label the four products with the names in the four adverts. Prepare or make up adverts for the products, for example:

Tired of scrubbing floors? Try new Eezi-Clean. Your floors will look like new! You'll be amazed!

Does your pet need more energy? Is he tired and unfit? Buy Doggo! Doggo puts the GO in dog! You'll notice the difference straight away!

Wrinkles? Ageing skin? Try Youthbright cream. Wrinkles will vanish in days .You'll look years younger

Are you tired of your evening meals? Do all your dishes taste the same? Get a Spice-pack and liven up your life. Three great new flavours. So easy to prepare! You'll be delighted!

Practise reading the adverts, linking words as shown. Practise your intonation: your voice should go up with the questions and down with the answers.

> **Comment**
> You can make the adverts easier or more difficult by adding or taking out words that link together. The decision should depend on whether your class is used to this kind of activity and how easy or difficult they find listening to English.

TIME GUIDE   45 minutes

Lead-in
1 Show the class one flashcard. Tell them it comes from an advert. Can they guess what it advertises? Collect suggestions, then put up all four flashcards and ask learners to discuss in pairs what they think is advertised in each picture. Use the pictures to pre-teach vocabulary that may be unfamiliar, for example, *wrinkles, scrubbing, energy*.

> **Comment**
> This lead-in activity has three purposes:
> 1 It gets learners' attention and helps to get them interested and curious about the topic.
> 2 Predicting the subject of the adverts will help them to understand when you 'perform' the adverts.
> 3 The pictures will help you pre-teach difficult vocabulary.

Introduce target language
2 Tell the class that they will hear four adverts. They should listen and match each product to the picture on the board. 'Perform' the adverts for the class, producing each product as you name it and holding it up to show the class.

Check comprehension
3 Go through the answers with the class. Ask some general questions to check their understanding:

What will happen when you use Eezi-Cleen?
What will happen when you use Youthbright?
What will happen when your dog eats Doggo?
What will happen when you use Spice-Pack?

> **Comment**
> The matching task and the questions direct learners to listen for the main meaning or 'message' of the adverts. More detailed understanding will come at a later stage.

Language focus: word linking

4 Take one advert. Repeat the sentences one at a time. Ask learners to count the number of words in each sentence. Go through, writing each sentence on the board, showing how the words are linked and how two or more words can sound like one.

> **Comment**
> The linking of words in connected speech causes learners problems in comprehension (i.e. listening) as well as problems in pronunciation. In teaching pronunciation, recognition, and production go hand-in-hand. In this lesson learners will work first on recognition and understanding then on production: pronouncing the phrases themselves.

5 Put up gap fill dictations for the rest of the adverts. Use gaps for the linked words and write the words which are unlinked, for example,

_____ _____ scrubbing floors? Try _____ _____-Clean. Your floors _____ _____ like new! You'll _____ _____!

Go through, showing how the words are linked.

> **Comment**
> Counting words and gap fill are good ways of focusing learners' attention on the way words are run together in speech. If exercises like this are repeated regularly, they will develop the skill of understanding the separate words instead of hearing them as all one word.

6 Check if the class knows why the words link together. Show them three examples:

Tired of
You'll look
Be amazed

If they need help, ask them how the first word ends and the second word starts. There are three answers:

Tired of: consonant + vowel
You'll look: same consonant
Be amazed: vowel + vowel.

Show them how when two vowels come together, a /w/ or a /j/ sound is put in to link them, for example, *puts the GO-w-in dog, be-y-amazed.*

| **Practise the language** | **7** | Repeat one advert for the class. Get them to repeat it, linking the words. |

> **Comment**
> One way to help learners to link words is to start with the consonant and vowel, for example, 'd' and 'o' to make /dɒ/, then expand the syllable outwards, for example, /dɒʊ/. Then finish with the two complete words, /ˈtaɪjədɒʊ/.

| **Language focus: intonation** | **8** | Show with a hand gesture how your voice goes up at the end of the questions, and down for the statements. As the class repeats, get them to use hand gestures to show the upward and downward movement of their voices. |

> **Comment**
> Hand gestures are a clear way of demonstrating intonation. Associating physical movement with intonation will help your learners produce and remember the right intonation.

| **Practise the language** | **9** | Put learners in pairs and get them to practise a performance of the adverts, one learner acting and the other doing a voice-over. |

Use the language **10** Write the following advert framework on the board:

_____? _____?	(start with questions)
Try/Buy/Get _____	(tell the customer to get your product)
_____!	(say something about the product)
You'll be _____	(tell the customer what will happen)

Now divide the class into groups of three or four. Give each group one of the household products and get them to work together to write an advert. They should mark in the linked words and intonation, and then practise it together, taking care with linking and intonation. When they are ready, groups can perform their adverts for the class.

2.5 Sample lesson 8

LEVEL Lower intermediate

LANGUAGE Syllables and word stress in adjectives:

Two syllables   **Three syllables**   **Four syllables**
dreadful   ex**cell**ent   fan**tas**tic   in**cred**ible
awful   **won**derful   a**maz**ing   as**ton**ishing
shocking   **ter**rible
awesome

Combinations of adjectives with **really**

What ... like?

The /ə/ sound in unstressed syllables

ASSUMED KNOWLEDGE Simple past, *wh–* questions, some adjectives for describing good and bad experiences

RESOURCES **Jazz chant:**

What was it **like?**	**Aw**ful!
What was it **like?**	**Dread**ful!
What was it **like?**	**Really bad!**
What was it **like?**	**Hor**rible!
What was it **like?**	**Ex**cellent!
What was it **like?**	Sen**sa**tional!
What was it **like?**	**Really good!**
What was it **like?**	**Won**derful!
What was it **like?**	A**maz**ing!
What was it **like?**	Fan**tas**tic!
What was it **like?**	**Really good!**
What was it **like?**	In**cred**ible!
What was it **like?**	**Ter**rible!
What was it **like?**	**Shock**ing!
What was it **like?**	**Really bad!**
What was it **like?**	**Hor**rible!

Flashcards of worst and best holidays

Best holiday
flashcards

Worst holiday
flashcards

Comment
The choice of pictures is important. The more dramatic the pictures
are, the more motivated the learners will be. You can find pictures in
magazines, on the Internet, in holiday brochures, and so on.

PREPARATION   Find or draw pictures of terrible and fabulous holidays. Make copies
of the jazz chant or make a poster for the front of the class.

TIME GUIDE   45 minutes

Lead-in   **1**   Show the class one fabulous holiday picture and ask, *What was this
holiday like?* Show them a terrible picture and ask what it was like.

Use the language   **2**   Put the class in pairs. Ask them to tell each other about the best and
worst holiday they have had. Ask them to talk about the food, where
they stayed, the weather, the people, and so on.

2.5 Focus on pronunciation

Introduce the language   3   Ask questions to individual learners: *What was the food like? What was the weather like?* etc. Put the adjectives they use on the board. Then add the adjectives listed at the beginning of this lesson. Ask the class which words describe best or worst holidays.

[Answers: best: excellent, wonderful, fantastic, amazing;
            worst: dreadful, awful, terrible, shocking, horrible.
            Incredible could be in either category.]

Language focus   4   Go through the first column on the board and ask the class to say how many syllables each word has and where the stress is. Get learners to work in pairs to do the same for the second column of words. A common sound in the unstressed syllables is /ə/. Say the words and get learners to raise their hands when they hear this sound (/ə/mazing, dreadf/ə/l, excell/ə/nt, unbeliev/ə/ble, wond/ə/f/ə/l, /ə/stonishing, terr/ə/ble).

> **Comment**
> The learners might need help with breaking words down into syllables. If so, say each word with the syllables separated, for example, *dread-ful*, *a-sto-ni-shing*.
>
> To help them with the word stress, say the word slowly and put an exaggerated emphasis on the main stress.

Check comprehension   5   Put the following symbols on the board

Get learners to clap the rhythm of each pattern with a loud clap on the big squares and a shorter quicker clap on the little squares. Invite learners to come to the board and write the words in each column:

dreadful	ex**cell**ent	fan**tas**tic	in**cred**ible
awful	**terr**ible	a**maz**ing	sen**sa**tional
shocking	**won**derful		
	horrible		

Get learners to say the words, clapping the rhythm as they say them.

> **Comment**
> Associating stress patterns with physical movement like clapping, tapping, or walking out the rhythm (with a stamp on the stressed syllables) is a good way of helping learners to understand stress and making it memorable.

Practise the language

6 Get learners to draw a 3 x 2 grid and to write one word in each square. Clap one of the four stress patterns from the board. If a learner has a word with the same pattern, they can cross it out. Repeat with more patterns. When a learner has crossed out all six words they can shout BINGO! They can repeat the game in small groups with one learner clapping out the words.

> **Comment**
> Bingo is a useful game for pronunciation practice. You can also use it to practise sounds, for example, learners choose six words from a list of minimal pairs like *long/wrong, liver/river, road/load, late/rate, rain/lane*. The teacher calls out words and learners cross them off as they hear them. They can also play in small groups with one learner calling out words.

7 Practise the jazz chant with the class. Hand out copies or put up a poster. Read the first four verses to the class, emphasizing the rhythm. You can get them to clap the rhythm along with you. Then get them to read with you. Divide the class in half down the middle. Get side A to ask the questions and side B to give the negative replies. Then side B asks the questions and Side A replies. You can go on to practise the next replies in the same way.

> **Comment**
> A **jazz chant** is a short rhyme or chant with a very strong beat. They should be spoken with an exaggerated emphasis on the stressed syllables. You can find out more in the book *Jazz Chants* by Carolyn Graham (see Further reading). Chants, songs, and rhymes are a lot of fun and an excellent way to practise stress and rhythm. The strong rhythm will help learners to get the right pronunciation and is also a memory aid, helping learners to remember new language.

Use the language

8 Put all the flashcards on the board. Tell the class that they have just come back from holiday and are talking to their friends. Ask the class what sort of questions the friend might ask:

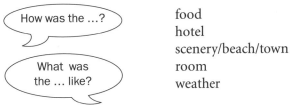

How was the ...?

What was the ... like?

food
hotel
scenery/beach/town
room
weather

Get learners to look at the pictures and choose five to answer the questions on the board. They can choose a wonderful holiday, a terrible holiday, or a mixture (for example, lovely place but awful weather). They should imagine they have just returned from this holiday. They should not tell anyone which pictures they have chosen.

Consolidation   **9**   When they are ready, put the class into new pairs to role play the conversation between the two friends. When they have finished the conversation, they should guess which pictures their partner chose.

3 Focus on skills

3.1 The structure of a skills lesson

What are skills?

Listening, reading, speaking, and writing are referred to as 'the four skills'. Listening and reading are **receptive skills**, i.e. they require only understanding. Speaking and writing are **productive skills**, i.e. they require the learners to produce something. For more details about each skill, see the introductions to sections 3.2–3.5.

How is teaching skills different from teaching language?

When you are teaching language, you are teaching 'what' (for example, a grammar point, a function, or a vocabulary item), and the aim of the lesson is to introduce and practise new language. When you teach skills you are teaching 'how': how to listen in a more focused way, how to read more quickly and efficiently, how to speak more fluently, or how to write particular types of text.

Learners master skills by practice, in a similar way to other skills like playing the piano or swimming. You can give them practice in the whole skill or in subskills. Learners can practise the skill of reading in a general sense by, for example, reading a whole text and then answering a question, or they can practise various subskills, such as guessing unknown words, scanning for particular information, or predicting what will come next. These subskills, like practising scales in music or learning the stroke movements in swimming, help with mastery of the whole skill.

How do I teach a skills lesson?

The simplest way of structuring a skills lesson is in three stages:

Before the skills activity

Lead-in
The activities in this stage should engage the learners' attention and get them thinking about the topic they will be hearing, reading, writing, or talking about. For example:

- To introduce a reading text about festivals, you could ask learners about their favourite festival in their country.
- To introduce a story the students are going to listen to, you could show learners a picture and ask them to predict the story.
- To introduce a lesson on writing postcards, you could bring in postcards sent to you for learners to read.
- To introduce a discussion of childhood memories, you could show the class a photo of yourself as a child and tell them one of your own memories.

Language focus
You might also include a short language focus to introduce some key vocabulary or expressions.

During

Tasks
There will be a task or series of tasks that the learners have to carry out, for example:

- Reading a text about festivals and matching pictures to the descriptions of the different festivals.
- Listening to a story and arranging pictures in the order of the events in the story.
- Learners get a holiday postcard with a picture on the front. They have to imagine they are in that place and write a postcard on the back.
- Learners complete a questionnaire about childhood memories and discuss with a partner.
  There may be several tasks in this stage, particularly in the case of reading and listening, beginning with more general tasks and progressing to more detailed tasks.

After the skills activity

Language focus
After the learners have completed each task, you will need to go through the task carefully, checking understanding and giving answers in listening and reading lessons, and giving feedback/error correction in writing and speaking lessons. You may like to have a specific language study spot, doing more detailed language work on a reading or listening text, or giving learners more practice in a structure or function that they are finding difficult in a speaking or writing activity.

Transfer
Finally, you can use the skills activity you have just completed as a springboard into practising another skill. For example:

- Learners write about their favourite festival from their own country.
- Learners act out the story in groups.
- Learners exchange postcards and read them. They think of four questions to ask about the postcard writer's holiday. Then they role play meeting after their holidays and discussing them.
- Learners write about their strongest childhood memories. In groups they make wall posters with a collage of 'Our memories'. These are pinned up for other learners to read.

3.1 The structure of a skills lesson

	Lead-in	Language focus
Listening **'The new flat'**	The teacher shows the students some pictures of flats and houses. The learners discuss which they like best.	The teacher uses the pictures to teach two new words *hallway* and *study*. The learners will need to know these words to understand the listening.
Reading **'Mountain rescue'**	The teacher writes some words on the board: *blizzard* *tourist* *mountain* *helicopter*. Learners predict what the text will be about.	
Speaking **'Happy families'**	The teacher asks the learners: *What makes a happy family?* He asks them to think individually of three things that make a family happy and to write three words down.	
Writing **'Long black hair'**	The teacher describes one of the learners, without looking at her. The learners guess who is being described. The teacher puts up three magazine pictures on the board and gives the learners three descriptions. The learners match descriptions and pictures.	The learners look at how the three descriptions are structured, making observations on the order of adjectives, for example: 1 Overall impression (height, size, age), then finer details (hair, face). 2 Most striking thing (bright eyes), then less obvious things. The learners look at ways of joining sentences using *and, with*, and *which*.

DURING

	Tasks
Listening **'The new flat'**	1 The teacher tells the learners they are going to listen to someone describing their new flat. He asks the learner to listen for how many rooms there are in the flat. He plays the tape twice and then checks the answer. 2 The teacher gives the learners a plan of the flat and asks them to listen again and label the rooms. He plays the tape again then gets learners to compare their answers in pairs. After playing the tape once more, he goes through the answers. 3 The teacher asks the learners to listen again and write in each room the colour it is painted. He gets them to check in pairs and then goes through the answers. 4 He plays a small section of the tape again and asks them to guess the words *balcony* and *French windows* by looking at their plan for clues. 5 He gives the learners a gap fill transcript of part of the tape, where the speaker runs words together. He asks them to listen again and write in the missing words. He plays the tape a number of times, and then goes through on the board.

Reading 'Mountain rescue'	1 The teacher shows the learners three headlines: *Mountain rescue, Tourist feared dead in mountains, Hunt for lost tourist.* She gives them a newspaper article and asks them to read the first sentence of each paragraph and then say which headline matches the story best. 2 She asks them questions about specific small details: the name of the mountain, the name of the tourist, and the date it happened. The learners search the text trying to find the answers as quickly as they can. 3 The teacher puts up five pictures of different events in the story in muddled order. The learners read the text and decide on the order of the pictures. They compare answers in pairs and then the teacher goes through the answers. 4 The teacher asks further, more detailed questions, for example: *Why was the tourist alone on the mountain? How did the helicopter find him?* The learners discuss in pairs and then the teacher goes through the answers, explaining anything that was unclear. 5 The teacher selects words from the text that describe feelings, such as *terrified* and *relieved*, and asks the learners to use the context to try to work out the meaning.
Speaking 'Happy families'	1 The teacher puts the learners in pairs and asks them to share their words and to say why they chose them. He then asks the pairs another question for discussion: *Is money necessary for happiness?* 2 The teacher puts pairs together into groups of four and gets them to share the previous two ideas. Then he asks another question for discussion: *Are children happier with strict parents or with easy-going parents?* 3 The teacher puts the learners into groups of eight and asks them to share the previous three ideas. Then the groups discuss three new questions: *What is necessary for a happy home?*, *What is not necessary (but perhaps desirable)?*, and *What makes an unhappy home?* 4 The groups report back to the class on their ideas. During all the above activities, the teacher circulates, listening to the learners talk and making notes on problem areas.
Writing 'Long black hair'	The teacher gives out magazine pictures and the learners write a description of their picture, using one of the texts as a model. The teacher circulates to help and check their progress.

AFTER

	Language focus	Transfer
Listening 'The new flat'	The teacher draws a mind map on the board. He asks the learners if they can remember any words the speaker used to describe the flat. The learners supply, for example, large, comfortable, and warm. The teacher asks if they know any more words for describing rooms and houses, and they give him some more words, for example, *light*. The teacher teaches them a few more, such as *spacious* and *cosy*.	The learners draw a plan of their ideal house, and then describe it to a partner.
Reading 'Mountain rescue'	Learners go through the text and highlight the time expressions such as *then, later that day*, and *by evening*, which show when and in what order the events happened.	The learners imagine they are the tourist and write a postcard home about their experience.

	Language focus	Transfer
Speaking '**Happy families**'	While listening to the learners, the teacher has noticed that they are having trouble with *If …* constructions, such as If the parents are too easy-going the children will get spoilt. He now uses sentences she heard them say as a grammar exercise, asking the learners to put the verbs in the right tense, for example: *If parents (be) too easy-going , their children (get) spoilt.* He goes through the sentences, explaining how they are formed.	The learners write a short essay on *What makes a happy family?*
Writing '**Long black hair**'	The teacher looks out for problems with adjective order and writes some examples on the board: 1 She was a tall thin girl. 2 He was a fat short man. 3 She had long dark curly hair. 4 He had black small twinkling eyes. They discuss which examples are correct (1 and 3) and which are not, and apply the order that they have observed to their own descriptions. The learners look through their writing again and correct any adjective order mistakes.	The teacher pins the pictures around the room and gives each one a number. She collects in the learners' descriptions and gives them out to different learners. Learners read their new description and go round the room to match it to the right picture.

3.2 Focus on listening

What does listening involve?

Listening is perhaps the most challenging of the skills to master in a second language. Although spoken language can be well organized and similar to written language, most of the time it is different from written text. A spoken conversation between several people is chaotic and complex, and there is no time to stop and go over something again, as you would if you were struggling to understand a written text. In English, speakers may miss out a subject or verb, or may break off their sentence in the middle, for example:

I was at the bus stop waiting for — when this car pulled up — it was Dave — offered me a lift ... well ...

A speaker may often hesitate to think about what he is going to say next, and plug this gap with fillers (little words or phrases like *um*, *you know*, *like*, and *I mean*), for example:

The play was, like, really long.

Speakers may also include words, phrases, or ideas that are not strictly necessary, or backtrack to correct what they have just said, often in the middle of a sentence, for example,

She's really beautiful — well not beautiful exactly, but interesting-looking — ...

Two speakers may overlap each other in a conversation rather than waiting for the other person to finish. The language used is often more colloquial (less formal) than written English, and is often more idiomatic. For example, asking someone to help you carry something, you might use, *Could you give me a hand?* rather than *I would be grateful if you could help me.* These features make listening difficult for learners, but there are ways you can train your learners to become better listeners.

How to help learners develop their listening skills

Teachers need to help learners recognize and deal with these features in several ways.

Focusing listening
Listening with a purpose
One way to do this is to encourage learners to think about why they are listening and exactly what information they are listening for. They can then adapt the way they listen to their aims. If learners try to process everything that they hear, they are constantly trying to

catch up with what someone is saying. So it is important that learners can focus their attention efficiently. We usually start by training learners to listen for the **gist** (general meaning) and not to worry about the details. For example, if we are listening to a story or anecdote, we are mainly interested in the sequence of events: what happened first, what next and so on. If the speaker makes digressions or includes unimportant details, we learn to ignore these and focus on the overall meaning.

Listening for gist
You can help learners to listen for gist by setting a question or task which you give to the learners before they listen so that they know what information they are listening for. An example is *Listen and match pictures to events in the story* in which case you would need to give the learners the pictures to look at before hearing the text.

Listening for specific details
Another way of listening is to listen for precise details. In everyday life we often listen for specific information, for example, which platform your train is leaving from, whether it is going to rain in your area tomorrow, so you learn to listen only for that information, ignoring the rest of what is said. Our learners need to learn how to listen for specific details in this way. You can give tasks that direct learners to listen for a specific piece of information, for example, *Listen to the airport announcements. Your flight number is PT346. What gate is your flight leaving from?*

Listening with a clear purpose in mind means that learners develop the ability to filter out everything they don't need to know.

These different ways of listening are illustrated in the listening lesson in 3.1, where listening for gist involves listening for how many rooms there are in the flat, and then listening for detail involves using the plan of the flat to label the rooms and listen for the colour of the rooms.

Dealing with unfamiliar vocabulary
However, another problem can be caused when learners simply don't understand the meaning of what is said and so are unable to tell whether the information is important or not. This may be because the vocabulary or the topic is unfamiliar. We can help learners with this in several ways:

Activating background knowledge
Because learners may have to listen to topics that are unfamiliar to them, it can be useful to introduce the topic and related vocabulary before doing a listening activity. For example, if they are going to

listen to something related to a country's political system, it would be useful to check whether they know who the prime minister or president is, how many parties there are, which party is currently in power, and so on. This activates any knowledge the learners already have and provides a context for listening.

Predicting
It helps learners understand if they think about the topic and try to predict what the speaker might say. This means they will have questions in their mind when they come to listen and this will help them focus their listening.

Pre-teaching vocabulary
It can help learners if you teach them some key words before they listen. You do not have to teach all the new words, just those which are essential for understanding the main meaning.

Guessing meaning
In everyday life people sometimes try to guess the meaning of a word they do not understand. If a speaker says, for example, *My partner and I are quite different. I always do things immediately but he always procrastinates* you might be able to guess what 'procrastinate' means by deducing it means the opposite of 'do things immediately'. It will help our learners if they can learn to guess or deduce meaning of unknown words from context in this way.

Two of these different ways of dealing with unfamiliar vocabulary are illustrated in the listening lesson in 3.1: the teacher pre-taught the key vocabulary *hallway* and *study*, because if the learners did not know these words they would not be able to do the second task of labelling the rooms in the plan. Later, the teacher asks learners to guess the meaning of *French windows* and *balcony*, which the learners can work out by looking at the plan.

Making sense of connected speech
Learners can also have trouble understanding because language is familiar in its written form, but sounds unfamiliar in speech. This is because of features like linking of words or insertion of fillers, which can make the words sound different. It is a good idea to choose a small section of the listening text to work on in detail to practise subskills in this way. In the listening lesson in 3.1 the teacher chose a few sentences from the listening where the words were run together and gave the learners a gap fill dictation. This helped them to identify the words and make sense of the sentence.

Identifying linked words
Identifying words in a stream of speech is an important sub-skill. Learners can practise this by activities like gap fill dictations or *Listen and count how many words*.

Identifying fillers
It is important for learners to know what little noises like *um* and *er* sound like, and to be able to recognize them as fillers, not as words with meaning. The teacher can do this with recognition activities such as asking the learners to raise their hands when they hear the fillers in a sentence.

Active listening
When we are listening to someone during a conversation we sometimes ask the speaker to repeat, explain, or slow down. We also use phrases like *Do you mean …?* and *Is that …?*, and so on. These are useful phrases for learners to know, and can help them to find their way when listening as well as to ask for clarification in their own conversations.

The stages of a listening lesson

Before: **Lead-in**: Engage learners' interest, introduce the topic and context, activate learners' background knowledge, help the learners to predict what the speakers might say, and introduce some key words and expressions.

Language focus: You may also want to introduce some key vocabulary. Other words can be left till later.

During: **Tasks**: You should aim to repeat the listening several times with a series of listening tasks. These should begin with tasks focusing on gist and then tasks involving more detailed listening. Learners may need to listen more than once for each task. After focusing on meaning you can work on sub-skills (guessing meaning, identifying words in connected speech, etc.). Remember to check comprehension after each task, and be ready to explain things that the learners did not understand.

After: **Language focus**: You might choose to focus on some of the language in the text, such as new vocabulary, expressions, or a particular structure or function.

Transfer: Use the listening and the language work as the basis for work in a different skill, for example, speaking or writing.

Selecting listening texts

Texts can be selected on the basis of interest, relevance, and level. In general, the listening text should be slightly above what can be easily understood by your learners. There is little value in learners listening to texts that they can understand immediately. A text that is too far above the level of the learners can be demotivating.

A more difficult listening text can be balanced with a relatively easy listening task, or vice versa. For example, an elementary class could listen to a more advanced text and just identify the situation, or pick out one or two details.

Learners should also have the opportunity to listen to a wide variety of texts:

Different text types
Listening should cover a range of different types of text, for example, conversations, announcements, talks, and stories.

Different situations
Listening texts should cover a wide variety of different situations, for example, at a station, asking directions, telephone conversations, panel discussions, and so on.

Levels of formality
There should be a range from formal to informal register, for example, a formal speech or a conversation between friends.

If you have access to the media and tape recorders the following are also important:

One- and two-way listening
Learners should have the opportunity for both one-way listening, to radio, television, or airport announcements for example, and two-way listening, as in conversations and discussions.

3.2 Focus on listening

Different accents

Remember that English is an international language, and has many varieties of accent and dialect. Consider which varieties and accents your learners are most likely to encounter, and try and use listening texts which reflect this diversity.

Different sources

If possible, learners should hear both tapes and teacher talk. Taped material will give learners exposure to a wide range of accents and speakers. If you do not have access to a tape recorder, you can invite other people to your classroom and improvise or act out conversations with them. Your own input is just as valuable though, as it provides two-way interaction. A conversation between you and your learners, or you telling them a story or anecdote from your own life, is in many ways more life-like than a taped conversation, since your learners can take part in and shape the conversation and you can react and respond to their feedback, as in real life.

Sample lessons: focus on listening

	Sample lesson 9	Sample lesson 10
Type of text	Answer phone messages	Story
Lead-in	Using pictures to teach key vocabulary and to predict content	Using flashcards to predict the story
Language focus	Key vocabulary in lead-in	Key vocabulary in lead-in
Task	Listen and complete (a diary) Listen and answer	Listen and answer Listen and draw Listen and order Listen and match
Sub-skill	Recognizing fillers	Identifying repetition Guessing unfamiliar words
Language focus	*Would like to …* for invitations	Adjectives for feelings
Transfer	Speaking game: invitations	Acting out television interviews

3.2 Sample lesson 9

LEVEL	Lower intermediate
SKILLS FOCUS	Predicting content Listening for meaning Listening for detail Identifying hesitation devices
LANGUAGE	Invitations: *Would you like to …?* and *Can you …?*
ASSUMED KNOWLEDGE	Vocabulary for leisure activities, for example, *concert, football match*; present simple, present continuous with future meaning, *Can*
RESOURCES	Board, cassette recorder (optional), cassette recording or transcript of answerphone messages.
PREPARATION	Record the messages if you have a tape recorder (see Stage 2). If not, practise saying them as naturally as possible, with hesitations.
TIME GUIDE	40 minutes

Lead-in

1 Begin to draw a picture of a telephone on the board. Ask learners to guess what it is you are drawing. Tell them that it is your telephone, and that you were out all day yesterday and when you came back there were four messages. Ask the class to predict what the messages might be. Use their suggestions to teach the words *invitation* and *appointment* if they do not already know them.

Listen for gist

2 Ask the learners to listen to the four messages. What are the four appointments? (dinner, dentist, football, jazz concert). Play the tape (or say the messages). Get learners to check in pairs, then go through the answers.

Oh er hi it's Tessa here erm … just wanted to um invite you over. Wanted to know … er … can you come to dinner on Tuesday? Sam and Jan are coming … Eightish? Er … about 8 o'clock … er… hope you can come.

This is to remind you your dentist's appointment is on Friday this week at 10.30. If there is a problem ring us back on 575 9194.

Oh er hello this is Pete. Er … just to ah … let you know er … the time is wrong on the tickets … the football match is at 3 on Saturday, not 2. I'll ring again tonight.

Ah … hi this is Sue … er, just to say … We're going to a concert — ah jazz concert — on Saturday — this Saturday — in the — It starts … I think it starts at 7 … no sorry … 7.30. Would you like to go with us?

3.2 Focus on listening

Listen for main meaning **3** Draw a diary on the board and ask learners to copy it.

Monday	Friday
Tuesday	Saturday
Wednesday	Sunday
Thursday	

Ask them to listen for WHO, WHAT, and WHEN (i.e. who is inviting, what the invitation is, and which days). They should write the invitations in the right days on the diary. Give them an example by writing *Film with Anna* in on Monday in the diary on the board. Rub it out again before they listen.

Ask learners to compare their answers in pairs. Ask one learner to come to the board. Play the tape or say the messages again, stopping after each one for the learner to fill in the diary.

Listen for detail

4 Ask learners to listen again and to write down the time next to the appointment in their diary.

> **Comment**
> This task focuses on extracting important information from the messages. It is done as a separate task because it is slightly harder than the previous task: the information is given in a confusing way—two messages mention two times: 3 *not* 2, and 7, *sorry*, 7.30. This means that learners will need to listen carefully to decide which is the right time. In real life, too, you might need to play the message again to check you have got the time right.

5 Repeat the messages again. Before each one give a question, for example,

Who else is coming to dinner at Tessa's?
What number do you ring if you have a problem with the appointment?
What was wrong with the football tickets?
What day is the concert?

Check the answers as before.

> **Comment**
> The listening activity gets the learners to listen for the finer details of the message. These details are not as vital as the information in the first two tasks.

Identify words

6 Explain that the messages are full of the little noises that people make when they stop to think what to say. Ask learners what they say in their own language. Then ask if learners noticed any in the messages. Write up on the board and add any they missed: *er, erm, ah, um*. Repeat the messages, asking learners to put up their hand when they hear the sounds. Dictate a few phrases, for example, … *just wanted to um invite you* …, asking learners to write the phrase leaving out the hesitation device.

> **Comment**
> This activity gives the learners practice in a sub-skill: learning to recognize hesitation devices. These little sounds can make listening difficult for learners as they are often run together with other words and change the way these words sound, for example, *to-um-invite-you* sounds like /tuːwʌmɪnˈvaɪtʃuː/.

3.2 Focus on listening

7 Ask learners what language the speakers used to make an invitation.

Write up:

> Can you   come to dinner?
> Would you like to   go to a concert?

Ask them to suggest more activities, for example, go to the cinema, go to a football match, and write these up. Then ask how you could reply. Write up some ways of replying, for example:

> Sorry, I'm afraid I can't, I'm …–ing then.

> I'd love to! That would be great!

Get learners to repeat, practising pronunciation.

> **Comment**
> This language will be directly useful in the speaking activity that follows.

Transfer

8 Get learners to sit in pairs back to back. Get them to imagine that one of them is ringing Tessa or Sue back to accept or refuse the invitations.

Get each learner to copy the diary and write in three activities (for example, *go to the cinema, go out for a meal*) on different days. Ask them all to stand up and walk around, asking other learners to come with them, accepting or refusing the invitation. When their diary is full they should sit down.

Get feedback from the class on the arrangements they have made for the weekend, and who managed to fill in their diary.

3.2 Sample lesson 10

LEVEL   Intermediate

SKILLS FOCUS   Predicting content
Listening for gist
Listening for detail
Guessing new words
Identifying repetition and reformulation

LANGUAGE   Vocabulary for emotions

ASSUMED KNOWLEDGE   Past tenses

RESOURCES   Handouts or poster of story transcript and sets of blank cards

PREPARATION   Prepare the blank cards (see Stage 5). Practise telling the story (see Stage 3). An outline of main events is given in the Lesson materials appendix on page 157, which you can use to help you tell the story, putting in some details of your own. Below the outline is an example of what an expanded version might sound like, told as naturally as possible for Intermediate/Upper intermediate learners.

TIME GUIDE   40 minutes

Language focus   **1**   Do a brainstorm with your learners. In the middle of the board put up this mind map.

Things that live in the sea

Things that you *do* in the sea

Get learners to provide you with any words they know, for example, *fish, octopus, swim, sail*. Write these up in appropriate places on the mind map. If a learner provides a word that the others may not know, ask him/her to explain. Miming or drawing is the easiest way to explain this vocabulary. Introduce some words of your own, making sure the words *dolphin, shark, seal,* and *surfing* are introduced at some point (though don't tell them they will come in the listening!).

> **Comment**
> The story involves suspense and drama. Telling the learners vocabulary from the text would give the story away. However, *shark, dolphin,* and *surf* are key words which they need to know. This brainstorm is a way of introducing this vocabulary, without giving away any secrets! It also provides useful language for the lead in discussion.

3.2 Focus on listening

Lead-in

2 Look at the list of things you can do in the sea. Get learners to discuss in pairs what they would like to do and what they would not like to do and why. Ask some learners for their opinions, for example,

TEACHER *Would you like to go diving, Antoine?*
ANTOINE *No!*
TEACHER *Why not?*
ANTOINE *It's dangerous!*
YUMIKO *But you can see some beautiful fish!*
ANTOINE *Yes — and horrible sharks!*

Listen for gist

3 The story you can use for the listening text can be found in the Lesson materials appendix on page 157.

> **Comment**
> Depending on the level of your learners, you can choose a level between the very simple language of the outline and the more difficult level of the expanded story. Even if you need to use simple language, you should try to make it sound natural, with some repetition, hesitation, and linking words.

Tell the class you are going to tell them a true story and that you want them to listen for the answer to two questions:

1 *What is the story about?*
2 *At the end of the story is the man dead or alive?*

> **Comment**
> This gives the learners a clear aim before they start to listen. At this stage they are not listening for all the details, but for the essential meaning: the main question in everyone's mind listening to this story will be — did the man survive?

Tell the story naturally, filling out the outline with lots of details and drama. Put the learners in pairs to discuss the answers to the questions, then go through the answers as a class. Encourage the learners to talk about the story.

> **Comment**
> Different learners will have understood and remembered different parts of the story. This activity gets them to share what they know and establish the main facts (man surfing — sees shark — dolphins save him—he survives).

Listen for main events

4 Ask learners to listen again and draw anything they hear. Tell the story again. Then put learners in pairs to compare what they have drawn and to explain their pictures to each other.

> **Comment**
> 'Listen and draw' is a good task for a story like this, with plenty of action and vivid images. You can also use it with descriptions, instructions, or directions.

Listen and sequence

5 Hand out six blank cards to each pair. Ask the learners to divide their story into six stages and draw a simple picture for each stage.

> **Comment**
> This gets the learners to think of the sequence of events and break them up into stages.

When they have completed the pictures, tell the pairs to write a sentence under each one describing what happened. Put the pairs into groups of four, and ask one pair to tell their story to the other pair. If the other pair has any cards that show an extra event or detail, they can add them in to the first pair's story at the right points. One group can come to the board and put up their pictures and tell the story to the class. If any other groups have a picture they could put in, let them come up and add the picture at the right point in the story.

Listen for detail

6 Put the following questions and word box on the board. Tell the story again and ask the learners to match the answers (from the word box) to the questions.

How did the man feel:

- when he realized he was far from land?
- when he saw the shark's fin?
- when he saw the shark in the water?
- when he saw the dark shapes?
- when the shapes came closer?
- when he realized it was a group of dolphins?
- when they surrounded him and led him to the shore?

> confused/ puzzled/ anxious/ terrified/ sick with panic/
> paralyzed with fear/ thought he was going to die/ amazed/ relieved

Guess words

7 Get learners to guess the meaning of words they don't know. You can help them by writing on the board the following definitions to match up with the words in the previous exercise.

> Didn't understand/ very surprised/ happy and thankful/
> very afraid/ worried

> **Comment**
> This matching exercise provides simple synonyms for the new words from the listening. It is a good technique for helping learners to guess meaning.

Identify repetition

8 Give learners the transcript of the listening task. This time they can listen and read at the same time, underlining parts where the speaker repeats an idea or says the same thing in different words.

> **Comment**
> It can be very helpful for learners to read and listen at the same time as a final activity. It helps learners make a direct relationship between words on the page and how they sound in connected speech. This particular task focuses on identifying all the repetition in the text, which the learners needed to ignore or filter out during the listening task.

Language focus

9 Get learners to look again at the list of words for feeling from stage 7. Ask them to discuss in pairs what they think the following people would feel:

- the man's wife
- someone watching from the beach
- another surfer.

Transfer

10 Put learners into groups of five or six to create a television interview. One should be the interviewer and the other should be the man involved. The rest should take the roles of the man's wife and family and people on the beach, in boats or in the sea at the time. Get them to prepare individually: the interviewer writing some questions, and the others working out their stories; what they saw, did, and felt. Then get them to perform their interviews.

> **Comment**
> This activity will give learners a chance to produce a lot of the language they heard in the story. Planning time gives them time to think out what to say and gives you time to circulate and help them if necessary. Planning is done individually, so there will be an element of surprise and freshness when they come to act out the interview: No one knows in advance what will be said.

3.3 Focus on reading

What does reading involve?

When you read in your own language, you read differently from the way you read in a foreign language. In our own language, we know how to focus our reading so that we concentrate on getting the main meaning from the text. We usually have a purpose for reading in our mind, which focuses our reading. If, for example, we were reading an article about a tourist lost in a blizzard, we would be reading in order to answer certain questions in our mind: *Was he rescued? How did he get lost? How many days was he lost? How did they find him?*

In our own language we use a variety of different ways of reading. We read in different ways depending on what we are reading and why. If we were reading a newspaper article, we might glance through it to get a general impression of what it is about before settling down to read again, in more detail. If we were reading the entertainment page in a newspaper to see what time a particular film is on, we would search the text for this specific information. If we were reading a magazine article, we might read it rapidly, for general meaning but if we were reading instructions — for example, a recipe in a cookbook, or a guide to using a new gadget — we would read every word and sentence.

We also use a variety of sub-skills to help us read efficiently. We use our background knowledge of a topic to help us predict the sort of information an article might contain. As we read, we also make predictions about what will come next. If we come to a word we don't know, we guess its meaning from the context. We use our knowledge of how different texts are structured to help us understand: we know that a story will contain a sequence of events, or that a newspaper editorial will have arguments for, arguments against, and a conclusion. Certain words act as signals to point out the structure of a text: A story will have words like *later*, or *the next day*, and an argument will have words like *however*, or *on the other hand*. These words signal to us when some new information is coming.

How to help learners develop their reading skills

You need to help learners to focus their reading so that they read for meaning instead of getting stuck on individual words or unimportant detail and losing track of the main meaning of the text. You need to help them read in different ways so that they can read different texts for different purposes. You need to help them to use sub-skills that will help them understand and improve their reading efficiency.

Focusing reading

As in listening, you can do this by encouraging learners to think about why they are reading and exactly what information they are looking for. Tasks or questions should direct learners to read for the main meaning. You can do this by setting comprehension questions or a reading task, like 'Read and match', or 'Read and draw'. It is important to suit the task to the kind of text. If you are reading a story, your attention will be focused on the events, what happened first, what next, and so on. Therefore, a 'Read and order' task will be appropriate here because it helps you focus on the sequence of events. If, however, you are reading a set of directions to someone's house, your attention will be on picturing the route you have to follow, so a 'Read and draw' task such as drawing a map of the route to your friend's house will be appropriate.

Reading in different ways

Skimming

If we want to get a general idea of what a text is about, our eyes focus briefly on a few words per line, perhaps headings, or the first and last sentences in a paragraph— these are the ones that should have the main point and conclusion. This is called **skimming**. We can give learners skimming tasks by giving them a very short time (maybe only 2–3 minutes) to look through a text to find the overall meaning.

Scanning

We also often scan a text to find a particular piece of information. To do this we move our eyes quickly over the text and only stop when we see the word or information we are looking for. We can practise **scanning** with our learners by asking questions about specific small details and giving a short time limit of 5–10 minutes to search for the answer.

Reading for gist

When we read for gist we read with a purpose in mind: questions we want answered about the text. We may skip some passages and read others more carefully.

Reading for detail

Some texts require very careful reading. When we are reading a legal document or a set of complicated instructions, we need to pay attention to all the sentences and to be able to follow the meaning of the whole text. This might also involve a certain amount of re-reading and checking words. When dealing with texts like these, we may want to give our learners questions which make them read more carefully.

You can give learners a series of tasks, so that they read in progressively greater detail. In the reading lesson in 3.1, the teacher used skimming, scanning, reading for meaning, and reading for detail tasks — in that order.

Extensive reading
When we read longer texts, such as novels, non-fiction, academic books, we may use a variety of the above ways of reading; reading some parts rapidly and others in greater detail. It is important to give learners extensive reading, where they read long texts for pleasure, as well as intensive reading, where they read a short text and practise reading skills.

Subskills
Activating background knowledge
As with listening, it helps learners understand if you can discuss the topic of the reading text with them before they read. Two useful techniques for doing this are brainstorming and mind-mapping.

Brainstorming means thinking quickly about anything related to a topic, for example, brainstorming 'Preparing for a holiday' might lead to the following ideas: *passports, packing, sun tan cream, foreign money, tickets, locking the house, calling family and friends*, and so on.

Mind-mapping involves putting ideas into some sort of order, for example into separate categories:

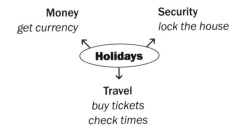

Doing this kind of activity before a reading task helps to activate any vocabulary learners already have and gives them a chance to add to this by putting together words and phrases from other members of the class. You can also use this opportunity to pre-teach key vocabulary.

You do not need to teach all the new vocabulary—just the words that are essential for understanding. In the reading lesson in 3.1 for example, the teacher made sure learners knew the meaning of keywords *blizzard, mountain, helicopter*, and *tourist* because without these, the text would be impossible to understand.

Here is a diagram summarizing what to do with new vocabulary in texts.

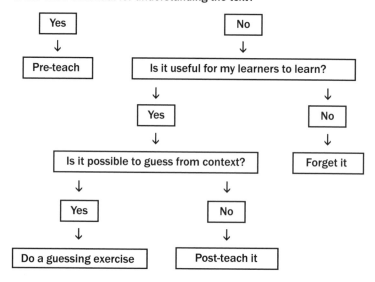

Predicting
In a similar way, learners can prepare for the topic they are going to read about by looking at titles and pictures, or words from the text. In the reading lesson in 3.1, the learners used the key words to predict what the text would be about.

We can also make mini-predictions all the time we are reading. When we read the beginning of a sentence: *It was only nine o'clock but Ally was tired so …* we predict as we read how the sentence will end: *she decided to go to bed.* It can help our learners if we give them some practice in thinking ahead as they read. We might, for example, give them the first sentence of a paragraph and get them to predict what will come in the paragraph.

Guessing new words
As in listening, this is a useful sub-skill to practise with learners. In the reading lesson in 3.1, learners guessed the meaning of 'feeling' words such as *terrified* and *relieved*. These words are not essential for understanding what happened and can be guessed from the context.

Using linkers
Some words act as signals to show us the structure of a text and help us to understand when a new bit of information is coming. These words are known as **linkers**. You can help your learners to become familiar with these signals which will help to point them to the main ideas. In 3.1 the teacher focuses on the linkers in the story which help us to understand when one event happens after another.

The stages of a reading lesson

These are similar to the stages of a listening lesson:

Before: **Lead-in**: In this stage you can engage learners' interest, introduce the topic and context, activate learners' background knowledge, and encourage the learners to predict what the speakers might say.
Language focus: You may also want to introduce some key vocabulary or expressions. This should be vocabulary that is essential for understanding the main meaning. Other words can be left till later.

During: **Tasks**: You should aim to repeat the reading several times with a series of tasks. These might begin with skimming or scanning, go on to tasks practising reading for main meaning and then go on to more detailed reading.
Subskills: You can also work on sub-skills such as guessing meaning, or identifying signals. Again you will have to check comprehension and explain after each activity.

After: **Language focus**: You might choose to focus on some of the language in the text: new vocabulary, expressions, or a particular structure or function.
Transfer: Use the reading and the language work as the basis for work in a different skill, for example, speaking or writing.

Selecting reading texts

The texts we choose for classroom use should:

Be interesting and motivating
It is obvious that learners will learn best if the reading material engages their interest.

Be appropriate to your learners' level
In general the intensive reading texts you work on in class should be slightly above your learners' level. If everything is easy for them, they will not be practising reading skills. However, extensive texts, such as simplified readers, should be a bit below your learners' level so that they can read fluently, for pleasure.

Have a variety of different text types
If your learners have a narrow focus, for example business English, then they will need texts that relate to their needs, for example business letters, reports, and so on. Other learners will need to have a range of different kinds of texts: letters, brochures, newspaper

articles, stories, advertisements, etc. You may like to include some **authentic texts** if you have access to them. 'Authentic texts' means texts that are taken from real life, such as newspaper articles, magazine articles, tourist brochures, advertisements, etc., and these are used so that learners should learn to read and listen to 'real' language rather than the artificial, simplified language of a textbook for learners. However, you need to be careful when choosing authentic texts: a lot them are is too hard for lower level learners. It is, however, possible to find authentic texts written in simple language: these would include advertisements, tourist information, and even simple recipes from a cookbook.

Include both extensive and intensive reading

Intensive reading means doing a series of tasks on a short text, usually in class time, where the teacher is on hand for questions and feedback. **Extensive reading** means using longer texts that learners read in their own time for enjoyment and to increase reading fluency. Graded readers—short versions of books simplified to suit learners at different levels—are an excellent way of providing extensive reading. If you do not have access to these, you can make a reading card scheme, by pasting texts onto card so that you have a lending library of reading cards. *Simple Reading Activities* (Oxford University Press) has instructions for making a reading card library.

Sample lessons: focus on reading

	Sample lesson 11	**Sample lesson 12**
Type of text	Story	Magazine article
Lead-in	Using pictures to teach key words and to predict content	Using key words to activate background knowledge and to predict content
Language focus	Key vocabulary in lead-in	Key vocabulary in lead-in
Task	Using pictures to teach key words and to predict content	Using key words to activate background knowledge and to predict content
Sub-skill	Predicting Guessing new words from context	Activating background knowledge Predicting Using linkers
Language focus	Simple past	*both/neither*
Transfer	Writing a strip cartoon	Speaking and group discussion

3.3 Sample lesson 11

LEVEL	Pre-intermediate
SKILLS FOCUS	Predicting content Reading for gist Reading for detail Guessing new words
LANGUAGE	Irregular pasts
ASSUMED KNOWLEDGE	Simple past
RESOURCES	Eight flashcards, story strips
PREPARATION	Draw the flashcards (see Stages 1 and 3) and prepare a set of eight story strips for each group of eight learners (see Stage 2).
TIME GUIDE	40 minutes

Lead-in

1 Show the class the first flashcard. Ask the class to describe the picture.

Use the picture to introduce the words *crocodile, jaws, hole, river,* and *riverbank*.

3.3 Focus on reading

Put the learners in pairs to discuss what they think will happen next. Collect suggestions from the class.

> **Comment**
> It is a good idea to introduce some key words before the learners read. You do not have to introduce all the new vocabulary—just the important words which are essential for the main meaning. If the learners can have a go at predicting the story before they read, this will help them understand the story. It does not matter if their predictions are right or wrong: what is important is that they have had a chance to think about the events in the story.

Read for gist 2

Why Dog is Man's Best Friend: A folk tale from Madagascar

One day a foolish man tried to cross a river at a place where there were a lot of crocodiles.

Suddenly a crocodile grabbed him and started to pull him to his hole in the riverbank.

The man was heavy and the crocodile was small so it was hard work! The man shouted 'Help, Help!' but there were no people around.

A dog heard the man's shouts. 'Hey, Crocodile, I'll help you and then we can share the meal,' she barked.

She dived in and helped the crocodile. Together they dragged the man onto the riverbank.

The crocodile opened his jaws to say, 'Thank you' to the helpful dog.

But quick as a flash the man ran off into the trees and the clever dog followed him, laughing.

And ever since that day Man and Dog have been the best of friends.

Put learners in groups of eight. Give each learner a story strip. (Give them out in muddled order.) Ask them to read out their story strip in turn.

They should decide on the order of events in the story and arrange themselves in the order of the story. (If you do not have enough space for learners to move around, you can group learners in fours, sitting round a desk and give two strips to each learner, or give one set of story strips to each pair and ask them to lay out the story strips on the desk and arrange them in order.)

> **Comment**
> When we read a story or a **narrative** with a sequence of events, the most basic and important thing to understand is what happened and in what order. This reordering activity focuses on getting the learners to understand the events in the story well enough to work out their sequence.

Check comprehension   **3**   Put up the flashcards on the board in order. Ask the learners to check the order of their story strips with the order of the pictures. Go through with the whole class, reading out a story strip for each picture.

> **Comment**
> The flashcards serve two purposes: 1 They show the learners the correct order of events and help them to check their own understanding. 2 The pictures will help the learners understand any events which were not clear to them before.

Read for detail   **4**   Put up these questions:

Why did the crocodile need help?

How did the man get out of the crocodile's jaws?

Why was the dog clever? Why was the man foolish?

> **Comment**
> This activity gets the learners to read for detail. These details help learners understand the story more completely and in more depth. The questions deal with cause and effect: why events happened and what the results were. This can be more difficult for learners to understand than understanding the order of events, so they will need to read more carefully to answer the questions.

Ask the learners to check in pairs, then go through the answers together as a class.

Guess words   **5**   Read again some parts of the text containing words the learners are likely not to know, for example:

The crocodile grabbed the man.
'I'll help you,' she barked.
The dog dived into the river.
They dragged the man onto the riverbank.
Ask learners to try to mime the actions. Explain any problems, showing with gestures what the words mean.

Language focus   **6**   Give the learners some gap fill sentences and ask them to complete them with the verbs in the past tense.

A man _____ to cross a river.

A crocodile _____ him and _____ to pull him to his hole.

The man _____ 'Help, help!'

99

3.3 Focus on reading

A dog _____ the man's shouts.

She _____ in and _____ the crocodile.

They _____ the man onto the riverbank.

The crocodile _____ his jaws to say 'Thank you'.

The man _____ off into the trees and the dog _____ him.

> **Comment**
> This activity practises focusing on accuracy of form when using the simple past, which will help learners when they come to write the story in the next activity. They can use the sentences as a basis for their story, adding to and elaborating them with phrases they remember from the story.

Transfer

7 Ask the learners to copy the eight pictures in the form of a strip cartoon.

Ask them to write a sentence below each picture telling the story and to add their own speech and thought bubbles to the pictures.

> **Comment**
> This activity gives some flexibility for learners to interpret in their own way. Weaker learners can simply retell the story using the framework in the previous activity to help them. Stronger learners can be more creative, adding phrases and ideas of their own, and using their imagination to create the thought bubbles.

3.3 Sample lesson 12

LEVEL	Pre-intermediate
SKILLS FOCUS	Predicting content Skimming Scanning Reading for detail Guessing new words
LANGUAGE	**both, neither**
ASSUMED KNOWLEDGE	Simple past
RESOURCES	Picture of identical twins (see Stage 1), reading text (see Stage 2), poster copy or handouts of the chart in Stage 4 (optional), whiteboard
PREPARATION	Make copies of the reading text (see Lesson materials appendix, page 158) or copy it onto a poster to put up at the front of the class, making sure your writing is big enough to be seen by everyone. Find a magazine picture of twins, or copy the pictures onto flashcards.
TIME GUIDE	40 minutes

Lead in

1 Show the picture of the twins to the class. Ask what the learners notice. Use the picture to teach *twins* and *identical*.

Write on the board, identical twin, separated, adopted, coincidence.

Explain the meanings to the learners and ask them to guess the story.

> **Comment**
> This text has a number of words that are hard for pre-intermediate learners. However the idea in the text is very simple and it will not be hard for the learners to understand either the main information in the text: the coincidence of the twins' similar lives, or the specific details: exactly what was similar. Some words like *astonishing* are not necessary for understanding the main meaning. Some, like *divorced* or *reunited* can be guessed from context. However, it would be hard to understand the text if you did not know what *twin*, *separated*, and *adopted* meant. These words are chosen for pre-teaching; learners will be asked to guess the others.

Skimming

2 Give out the reading text. Ask, *What is the story about?* Tell the learners to look very quickly all through the text. Give the students 30 seconds to look at the text, then cover it up. Ask them to turn to a partner and tell them what they think the story is about. Collect suggestions from the whole class.

Now ask the learners to read only the first and last sentences of the text. Cover the text again and ask them what happened to the twins.

> **Comment**
> A time limit will help learners develop the skill of skimming rapidly through a whole text just to get a very general impression. Other good ways of getting an overall impression of what a text is about are reading the first and last lines or, in longer texts, the first and last paragraphs, or the first sentence of each paragraph.

Scanning

3 Ask the learners short questions about specific facts. Do not go through the text in order, but jump around, for example,

Were the twins adopted by the same family?

When were the twins separated?

How old were the twins when they met for the first time?

Where were the twins born?

> **Comment**
> In scanning tasks, the learners develop the skill of hunting for specific details. They look through a text rapidly, searching for the right information and ignoring the rest. It is important to give them questions scattered throughout the text, not in the order in which the answers come in the text so that they develop the skill of glancing quickly through whole texts, not reading line by line. The answers to questions will give the learners important background information about the twins: the fact that they were separated at birth, lived separate lives, and did not meet for 40 years. This will provide a context for understanding the details in the next activity.

Read for detail

4 Give out the chart or put up the chart and get learners to copy it. Ask them to fill it in with information from the text. To help them find the information, you can ask them first to glance through and circle the word *both* each time it appears. This word acts as a signal showing when new information is coming. Get learners to check in pairs then go through the answers. Discuss their reactions:

How did they feel when they read about the coincidences?

Do they know any twins? Do surprising things happen to them?

Has anyone ever had a coincidence?

	Twin 1	Twin 2
name		
jobs		
good at		
first wife's name		
second wife's name		
son's name		
dog's name		

Comment

This is a simple task which directs the learners to read for the exact details of the coincidences. The learners will probably want to talk about the text when they have understood these details, giving their reactions or perhaps talking about a coincidence that happened to them.

Guess words

5 Read again some parts of the text containing words the learners are likely not to know, for example,

*Identical twins often have **astonishing** stories.*

*There were some amazing **coincidences**.*

*They both **divorced** their wives and married again.*

*Forty years later the brothers **were reunited**.*

Ask them to guess the new words: can they think of a word they know to replace the new words? Put them in pairs to discuss, then write on the board,

Met again   separated from   very surprising

Ask learners which words these could replace.

Language focus

6   Ask learners to look back through the text and find the words *both* and *neither*.

Write the table below on the board for learners to fill in with the phrases from the text:

Neither	Both
_____ _____ the boys	_____ _____ the boys
_____ _____ them	_____ _____ them
_____ family	_____ families

Ask, *When can you use* them, us *and* you? (Answer: *with* neither/both of …), *When is the used?* (Answer: *with* neither/both of …), *When is it not used?* (Answer: *with* neither/both …).

> **Comment**
> The text contains a lot of examples of *neither* and *both* so it is an obvious choice to focus on this piece of language. The table is designed so that when learners have filled it in from the text, it will summarize the way we use *neither* and *both*. This focus on language gives a basis for the speaking task which follows.

Transfer

7   Put learners in pairs. Tell them they have a time limit of five minutes.

They have to write down as many sentences about themselves as possible, beginning

Both of us …
Neither of us …

For example, *Both of us have four brothers. Neither of us likes fish.*

The sentences must be true!
Can they find any coincidences? At the end, get the pairs to report back to the class.

3.4 Focus on speaking

What does speaking involve?

Learners need to be able to interact with other people. This involves a wide range of skills.

First of all, they need to think of something to say in the second language and feel confident enough to try to express it.

Then they have to put words phrases and sentences together — using grammar and vocabulary — to express what they want to say in a way that others can understand. They have to be able to vocalize this — using pronunciation and intonation—in a way that is clear enough for others to understand. In order to do all this quickly enough to keep up the flow of conversation they need to be reasonably fluent.

They may also have to stretch the language they know to cope with new situations: instead of hesitating to search for a word they have forgotten or don't know, they need to be able to find another way of expressing their meaning.

Interaction involves more than just putting a message together; it involves responding to other people. This means choosing language that is appropriate for the person you are talking to. It means responding to what they say, taking turns in a conversation, encouraging them to speak, expressing interest, changing the topic, asking them to repeat or explain what they are saying, and so on.

How to help learners develop their speaking skills

We can help learners speak by helping them to find ideas and supporting them so they feel confident enough to speak. We can give them opportunities to practise enough to become fluent, and we can get them to improvise and stretch the language that they know to cope with a range of different situations. We can give them opportunities to interact with others and help them with useful phrases and expressions for turn-taking, changing the topic, expressing interest, etc.

Finding ideas
Learners need help in finding things to say. If you come into your class and announce, *Today we are going to discuss Climate change*, unless you have a very responsive class, you may be met with blank stares and tongue-tied learners. Alternatively you may get one or two learners who are willing to speak, while the rest remain silent. There are several ways in which you can help learners get over this problem of 'I don't know what to say.'

3.4 Focus on speaking

1 Provide some initial input in the form of a short reading passage or listening text on the topic. This will contain some useful vocabulary, and can get students thinking around the topic and stimulate ideas.

2 Provide help with what to say. You can provide learners with role cards or information cards which give them an outline or suggestions of what they can say. They can then expand the ideas on the card, adding ideas of their own.

3 Set a precise task. It helps if there is a goal or final outcome rather than an open-ended discussion. Examples of goal-oriented tasks you could set are:

- discuss arguments for and against a topic and come to an agreement.
- discuss a problem, such as how to design a house you would all like to live in, and find a solution.
- share information to complete a task, such as finding the differences between two pictures.
- fill in a questionnaire and compare your answers with a partner to find similarities and differences.
- role play a discussion, for example between members of a family deciding what television programme to watch, and come to a decision.

4 Break the task down. A general discussion question can seem daunting, but if you break it down into smaller questions, this makes it easier for the learners. One technique for doing this is called a **pyramid discussion**, where learners are given a series of small questions and work first in pairs, then groups of four, and then groups of eight. You can see this in the Speaking lesson in 3.1. Other ways of breaking discussion tasks down are by using questionnaires or ranking activities like the one in Sample lesson 13.

Developing confidence

Learners who are shy to speak in their own language may find it even more difficult in a new language. You can help develop their confidence in several ways:

1 Give planning time. If learners are given time to have ideas and think out what they want to say, this will help them to feel more confident.

2 Let the learners warm up by sharing ideas in pairs before they have to speak in a group or to the class.

3 Use activities where everyone has to participate in order to achieve the outcome. Information gap activities like the one in Sample lesson 14 are a good example of this: each student's information is necessary to complete the task.

4 Build in repetition. Repeating something a second time will give the learners more confidence and fluency. For example, a pyramid discussion gives learners the chance to summarize their ideas to different partners before going on to discuss a new question.

Developing fluency

Learners learn to speak by speaking. This means we need to give them plenty of opportunities for communicating in different situations and on different topics. To develop fluency, learners need as much practice as possible. This means organizing the speaking lesson to give them as much opportunity to speak as possible and getting learners to work in pairs and groups rather than in teacher–student interactions.

Monitoring and feedback

It also means taking a back seat while they speak. Interrupting learners to correct them while they are speaking means that they will not get the chance to develop fluency. Speaking practice is a good time for you to listen to the students and monitor their progress. You can then plan further language work according to their needs. You can do this directly after the speaking activity, by giving feedback on errors. You can deal with errors in various ways, for example by writing up sentences on the board and asking learners to 'Spot the error', or by including a mixture of correct and incorrect sentences and getting learners to sort them out. As you gain confidence in listening for errors, you can keep cards for individual learners and write notes to help them, for example:

FEEDBACK CARD: CHEN MEI

22/03   It was very bored for me.

Look up the difference between bored and boring in your dictionary. Write sentences about yourself using these words: bored, boring, interested, interesting, excited, exciting.

You can also do a grammar exercise that focuses on errors that the learners were making, or if many learners are having the same problem, you can plan your next lesson or lessons around language that the learners were finding difficult or getting wrong.

Stretching language

In Section 2.5 we looked at various speaking activities that practised new language. In this section we will look at activities that get learners to use the language they already know to communicate with others. This is important to help them become more fluent speakers. Using English outside the classroom, learners will not be in a predictable situation where language is selected and controlled. Speaking activities give them practice with these more demanding situations: they form a bridge between the classroom and the real world, helping learners to push their language knowledge to the limit to cope with a range of different situations.

Interacting

Learners interacting in pairs or groups may need some help with typical language we use for turn-taking in conversations. They may need to know how to interrupt politely, how to disagree politely with what someone is saying, how to go back to an earlier point in the conversation, and so on. It will help them if you can introduce expressions like *Could I just say something here?*, *That's an interesting point but …*, and *Could we go back to what you said about …*

The stages of a speaking lesson

A speaking lesson follows the same *Before/During/After* format as other skills lessons:

Before: **Lead-in**: Introduce the topic. It helps if you can give the learners some input which will provide them with ideas: a brainstorm around the topic or a short introductory listening or reading text.
Language focus: You can also introduce key vocabulary and useful expressions.

During: **Preparation**: Set up the speaking task with clear instructions. Learners work in pairs or alone to brainstorm ideas and plan what to say.
Speaking task: Learners work in pairs or groups to carry out the task. While they do this you can circulate, listening to the learners to see how they are doing. You can make notes of errors and areas of difficulty for feedback later.

After: **Language focus**: Here you can focus on problem areas and error correction.
Transfer: You can follow up the speaking task with a writing activity.

Selecting speaking tasks

Level

The tasks you choose should be at the right level for your class. An elementary class will be able to cope with a simple discussion, such as favourite food, or a simple role play, such as deciding what to do at the weekend, but would find it hard to cope with an in-depth discussion on heavyweight topics such as *Pollution* or *Smoking in public places*. However, many speaking tasks can be adapted to a range of levels. A discussion on what kind of surprise birthday treat to organize for a friend could be adapted to different levels with elementary students producing language like *Let's go to a concert. She likes jazz* and more advanced learners producing *Well, we could take her to a concert but would she prefer a party?*

Interest and variety

You should also choose speaking tasks that are interesting, motivating, and fun for your learners.

You should aim to provide a variety of different tasks. Some will appeal to some learners more than others: some learners might prefer 'serious' discussions, others might prefer lighter-hearted activities like games and role play. You need to provide a balance to cater for all your learners, but also to provide a range of different kinds of speaking:

- discussion and argument around various topics of interest
- social conversation (for example, inviting people round)
- conversations about personal feelings, experiences, and preferences (for example, childhood memories, or where you would like to live)
- factual information (for example, describing a person)
- transactional language (for example, making enquiries at a railway station).

Sample lessons: focus on speaking

	Sample lesson 13	Sample lesson 14
Type of activity	Discussion	Role play
Lead-in	Reading text supplies context and ideas for discussion	Role play cards give the learners something to say
Stimulus	Reading text supplies context and ideas for discussion	Role play cards give the learners something to say
Preparation: confidence boosting	Learners work alone to rank ideas	Learners work in pairs to prepare story
Task	To agree on three ideas	To solve mystery
Repetition	Learners regroup to share ideas discussed in the first group	Learners talk to each other to retell story to several different learners
Participation	Interaction strips game encourages learners to speak	Information gap activity means everyone must speak. Everyone must communicate information in order to solve mystery
Language focus	As needed by students	As needed by students
Transfer	Students write a manifesto stating their views	Students write newspaper article

3.4 Sample lesson 13

LEVEL	Intermediate
SKILLS FOCUS	Extended speaking Interaction
LANGUAGE	Giving opinions
ASSUMED KNOWLEDGE	Social problems and places in town; language for giving opinions
RESOURCES	Leaflet or poster 'Interaction' handouts— slips of paper with phrases that are useful in an interaction, for example:

> Sorry, I couldn't catch that.
> Do you mean …?
> Could we go back to the point about …?
> Could I just say something here?
> Could you explain that (a bit more)?
> I'd like to mention/talk about …
> That's all from me.

You will need copies of each expression so that there are five copies of each phrase for each group.

PREPARATION	Prepare the leaflet used in Stage 3 (Speaking preparation): the text can be presented to the learners either as a role card for each learner or as one copy on a big sheet of paper for the front of the class.

Prepare the interaction handouts (see Stage 6)

Look at the vocabulary in Stage 2 (Lead-in/Language focus) and think about how you would teach each word: would you mime, draw, or explain them?

TIME GUIDE	40 minutes

Lead-in

1 Ask learners to think of the town they live in. What problems are there? What one improvement would they like to have in the town? Collect suggestions.

> **Comment**
> Getting the learners to relate the topics to their own lives makes the lesson more relevant and interesting. Thinking about their own town will activate background knowledge and make reading the article easier.

Language focus

2 Put up the following words on the board:

suburbs	office blocks
traffic jams	hospital
overcrowding	leisure centre
crime	arts centre
unemployment	schools

Tell the learners the words come from a public information leaflet for people who live in the local area. Ask them to divide the words into two groups:

Places in a town   *Problems in a town*

Mime, draw, or explain any unfamiliar words.

. . . .

Speaking preparation   **3**   Give out the text or put up the poster (see Lesson materials appendix, page 158). Ask learners to read the text and then to number the improvements in order according to how they think the money should be spent.

> **Comment**
> The newspaper article provides a context for the speaking task. It also is a source of ideas, vocabulary, and expressions. The ranking activity (numbering the improvements) allows the learners some thinking time to work out their opinions and their reasons for what they think, before they have to speak.

. . . .

Speaking task   **4**   Put learners in groups of four. Ask them to present their ideas. The group should come to an agreement on three improvements they think are most important.

> **Comment**
> This activity has an end point—agreeing on three improvements. Specifying an outcome like this means that the discussion will be more focused.

. . . .

Speaking preparation: discussion   **5**   When the group have reached agreement, let them make a name for themselves according to the ideas they support, for example, 'Fight Crime' or 'Youth Energy'. Tell them they have to fight for their ideas. Give them some preparation time to think of more arguments to support their opinions.

. . . .

Language focus   **6**   Regroup the learners into new groups. The easiest way to do this is to give everyone in each group a number 1–4. Then get them to re-group so that all the 1s are together, all the 2s are together, and so on.

> **Comment**
> Regrouping is a useful technique. It allows learners to prepare ideas together with people in one group, then move to a different group, where everyone will have different ideas. They will benefit from having the chance to repeat their ideas in a different context and to hear new ideas from the members of the new group.

Hand out the 'interaction' slips so that each group has five copies of each phrase. Explain that each time someone uses a phrase correctly they take a slip. The person with the most slips wins.

> **Comment**
> In this lesson the learners are encouraged to use the expressions by making the activity more of a game. This means that the learners are motivated to try out the language. However, it is fine if they choose not to as long as they are actively participating in the discussion.

Check comprehension

7 Discuss with the class when they would use each phrase, for example:

TEACHER   *Let's look at the next phrase, 'Could we go back to the point about …?' When do we use this? Anyone?*

ANATOLY   *We want to talk about something before.*

TEACHER   *Right. We want to go back to something.*
The next one – 'Sorry. I couldn't catch that'?

MARIA   *We want to hear it again.*

TEACHER   *So 'catch' means …?*

MARIA   *'Hear'?*

Speaking task

8 Set the new task: everyone must try to persuade the rest of the group to agree with their ideas. They should each present their ideas in turn. After each person has spoken, the others can comment and argue, using the interaction slips. Set a time limit of about 15 minutes for this task. At the end there will be a vote.

Get each group to vote on the three things they think should be done first. Then take a class vote (each group can vote for the three improvements it finally decided on).

Transfer

9 Ask groups to write a short 'manifesto', explaining what three improvements they chose to spend money on and why.

3.4 Sample lesson 14

LEVEL	Intermediate
SKILLS FOCUS	Speaking: improvising speaking from role cards
	Reporting events, describing people
LANGUAGE	Narrating past events: past simple, past continuous
ASSUMED KNOWLEDGE	Describing people's appearance
RESOURCES	Role play cards (see Lesson materials appendix, page 159)
	Reading handout (police report, see Lesson materials appendix, page 160)
	Flashcards
	An A4 sheet of paper for writing down errors (see Stages 3 and 6)
	Scissors (see Stage 6)
PREPARATION	Make enough copies of the eight role cards in Stage 2 (Speaking preparation) for everyone in the class to have one. Make copies (or a poster) of the police report in Stage 4.
	Look at the vocabulary in Stage 1 and think about how you could teach each word: would you mime, draw, or explain them?
	Make 6–8 flashcards with simple drawings of men for your 'ID parade' in Stage 5. The flashcards need to include one man with a big nose and dark hair, one short man with glasses, one tall man with a beard, and one with long hair in a ponytail and a tattoo.
TIME GUIDE	50 minutes

Lead-in

1 Put up the following words on the board

masked   *held up*
robbers   *security guard*
registration number   *at gunpoint*

Tell the learners the words come from a police report. Mime, draw, or explain any unknown words. Ask the learners to work in pairs and guess what happened. Discuss their ideas as a class.

Speaking preparation

2 Divide the class into groups of eight. If you have learners left over, put one of them with each group of eight — for example, if you have a class of 36 learners, make 4 groups of 8 and then put one extra learner with each group. Give one set of eight role play cards to each group.

Give an extra card to the 'extra' learners: it does not matter which card you give them.

> **Comment**
> This is a kind of 'information gap' game: the learners have different information and need to share this information in order to achieve the goal, in this case to find out what really happened. Learners have to role play different characters, but it is not important for them to actually 'act' in character (unless they want to)—just to convey their information.

In each group, get the learners to work in pairs: 1 and 2 together, 3 and 4 together, 5 and 6 together, and 7 and 8 together. Get the learners to discuss what they 'saw' and develop their stories, for example, by saying how they felt, and adding details without changing the basic information.

> **Comment**
> With this sort of lesson it is important to have everything organized before the lesson. Work out how you are going to group your learners, and how many cards you will need. Sort the cards into sets (different coloured paper is useful for this) and make sure that you keep them safe by paper-clipping them in sets or securing each set with an elastic band.

Speaking task: role play game

3 When the pairs have had 5–10 minutes preparation time, begin the role play. Ask the groups to stand up, and talk to as many people in their group as possible to find out what they saw and to try to work out what happened. You can set a time limit for this stage, for example, 15 minutes.

> **Comment**
> **Mingling activities** like this, where learners move around and share their information with several other learners, give the learners lots of practice. Repeating their story several times to different people will help to boost their confidence and fluency.

While the role play is going on, don't interrupt but take notes yourself on any difficulties. Write the incorrect sentences or phrases on a sheet of paper that you can cut or tear up later.

Share information

4 When the time is up, ask learners to sit down again with their original partner. They should discuss what they learnt from the other 'witnesses'. Give them a few minutes to do this and then give out the police report or put it up as a poster. Ask the pairs to work together to find the mistakes in the report.

> **Comment**
> In an information gap activity it is important that the learners have an
> opportunity to check the information they have been talking about. It
> gives them and you a chance to judge how successfully they have done
> the activity and for the learners to find out the right answers.

When the pairs have corrected the police report as far as they are able,
ask them to work with the whole group of eight to check their
corrections. Finally go through, reading out the report and asking
learners to shout *STOP!* when there is a mistake and to tell you the
correction.

Describe people

5   Tell the class that the police know which plane the robbers are on.
    It has not landed yet. If they can get a description of the men to the
    police in Spain, they can arrest the men when they arrive. Put up the
    flashcards, like an identity parade. Which group can identify the four
    men first?

Language focus

6   Cut the piece of paper with the errors (from Stage 3) into strips with
    one error per strip. Give one strip to each pair of learners and ask
    them to find the mistake. Go through the errors with the whole class.

Transfer

7   Ask learners to write a newspaper article about the robbery using
    facts they learnt from the other witnesses and from the corrected
    police report.

3.5 Focus on writing

What does writing involve?

Writing is a difficult skill for many learners, even in their mother tongue. There are several reasons for this. First, writing has to be learnt, unlike speech, which is acquired in the mother tongue as part of a child's normal development. In addition, speaking is a familiar everyday activity, but for many people writing is something they do only rarely.

Another difficulty is the problem of the absent audience. When we speak, we are interacting with someone and have instant feedback on whether the information we are giving is what the hearer needs to know, whether it is clearly expressed and whether it is interesting. When we write we cannot consult with the reader. It is difficult to know what information the absent reader needs to know, and so it is hard to know what to write. This difficulty is even worse with classroom writing. At least in real life we usually know why we are writing and who we are writing to (or for). In the classroom these questions are often left unanswered.

Then there are linguistic difficulties. The writer has to know how to put a sentence together accurately. Writing tends to be either more elaborate than speech, with more lengthy constructions:

> The council will vote tomorrow on the controversial city centre redevelopment but, when asked about the likely result, councillors last night refused to predict how the vote might go, saying that the public would be able to express their opinions to the council before the debate began, and that this might affect the outcome.

or more condensed than speech, in the case of notes, texts, headlines:

Police arrest four in raid on house

DINNER IN FRIDGE

Mum

Some linguistic difficulties have to do with knowing what is appropriate language for different types of writing. This may involve knowing the conventions of particular types of text, for example that a business letter begins with *Dear Sir* and ends with *Yours faithfully*, or it may involve knowing what is the right level of formality, for example, that a colloquial expression like *It was great!* would be acceptable in a letter to a friend but not in an academic essay.

Another difficulty we have when writing is how to organize and sequence our ideas. Writing involves more than putting sentences together in language that is grammatically correct and appropriate. The ideas in those sentences need to be organized in a logical way so that they make a coherent text which is easy for the reader to follow. When we speak, our ideas often come out in a jumbled, confused, or incomplete form, and our listeners can help us by asking us to repeat, explain, or clarify. In writing we have to get it right first time! For example, when we read the following text, it is hard to get a clear picture of the girl:

> Lucy had long legs. Lucy's eyes were blue. Lucy had long hair. Lucy's arms were long. Lucy's hair was brown. Lucy was tall. Lucy looked awkward. Lucy's face was pale. Lucy was thin.

The following description, however, makes it much easier for the reader to picture Lucy.

> Lucy was a tall, thin, awkward-looking girl with long legs and arms. She had a pale face with blue eyes and long brownhair.

The writer has made the text more coherent by organizing the description so that we get overall impressions first, followed by smaller details. This follows the order in which we would notice things if we actually saw Lucy.

The writer has also made the text easier to read by linking the ideas together with *with* and *and*. This way of linking ideas in text is called **cohesion** and the words that link ideas are called **linkers**. They signal the different logical connections between one idea and the next: words like *and* or *moreover* signal to us that a new fact or idea is about to be added. Words like *but, however,* and *in contrast* signal that a new idea or fact is coming which will contradict the previous one. Words like *so* and *therefore* signal that one thing happened as a result of another.

Another way ideas are linked in text is by use of **back reference**: in the description above the writer used *she* to refer back to Lucy instead of repeating the name again.

To sum up, the writer has to answer these questions:

- Why am I writing?
- Who am I writing to (or for)?
- What have I got to say?
- How can I express my ideas:
- – appropriately?
- – accurately?
- – clearly?
- How can I organize my ideas in a logical sequence?
- How can I link my ideas together so that my writing flows smoothly?

How to help learners develop their writing skills

When you teach writing you can show the learners how to produce a particular text type, for example a thank you letter, a business report, or an article, by providing examples of the type of text and helping the learners to see how they are structured and what language is typical of that text type. This is called **genre-based writing**. You can also focus on the stages a writer goes through to produce text: for example brainstorming ideas, writing a draft, and editing. This is called **process writing**.

Genre-based writing

When you teach learners how to write a particular type of text you can give them activities to practise accuracy, give them guidance in what to say and how to say it, or allow them to write completely freely. These three different types of activity can help learners with their 'writer's questions' in different ways.

Accuracy activities
Accuracy activities involve a range of writing exercises such as gap fill, reordering sentences, combining sentences with appropriate linking words, matching topic sentences and paragraphs, or rewriting texts. These exercises can help students develop the skills of linking ideas between sentences (cohesion), choosing suitable language (**appropriacy**) and organizing the structure of the text as a whole (**coherence**) as well as improving grammatical accuracy. The following exercise, for example, practises both coherence and cohesion:

Reorder the sentences to make the story clearer. Then combine some sentences to link the ideas.

Use these words: *because/so/as*

Are there any other changes you need to make to avoid repeating words?

A dog stole a piece of meat. He wanted to eat it at home. He had to cross a river. He started to carry the meat home in his mouth. He went onto the bridge. He looked down into the water. He saw another dog in the river. The dog had a piece of meat. He wanted that piece of meat too. He opened his mouth. His piece of meat fell into the river. He tried to bite the dog. He went home with no meat.

(Adapted from Aesop's *Fables*)

The corrected version:

A dog stole a piece of meat. He wanted to eat it at home so he started to carry the meat home in his mouth. He had to cross a river and as he went onto the bridge he looked down into the water and saw another dog in the river, who had a piece of meat. He wanted that piece of meat too so he opened his mouth to bite the dog. His meat fell into the river, and so he went home with no meat.

There is an example of an accuracy activity in Sample lesson 15 (Stage 4).

Guided writing
Guided writing involves giving learners some help with the questions What have I got to say? and How can I organize my ideas? (coherence). Some ways you can do this are by:

- giving a series of pictures that tell a story and asking the learners to write the story
- providing outline notes or key words
- giving a 'model text' so that learners can see an example of the kind of writing they are expected to produce and use it as a pattern for their own text. You can help them by pointing out language that is commonly used in that type of text.

Sample lesson 15 uses a model text for guided writing.

Free writing
Free writing is the most difficult task for learners. A task like *Write a story for homework* or *Write a letter to a newspaper* gives them no help with any of their 'writer's questions'. However, there are some ways we can help them with free writing, while still leaving them the choice of what they write and how they express and structure their writing.

a Provide a stimulus
We can help them with the question of what to write by providing a stimulus. Pictures, music, and realia can help to stimulate the learners' imagination. For example, pictures of people could provide inspiration for a character description; listening to a piece of music could inspire a story or a poem; and a collection of objects (such as a train ticket, a love letter, a ring, and a photo) could inspire a story.

Listening or reading input before the writing activity can provide the learners with ideas: listening to a news broadcast could provide them with ideas for writing a newspaper article; or reading a letter from a magazine 'problem page' could provide a stimulus for writing a letter of advice.

Holding a class or group discussion or role play can help learners develop ideas and rehearse them in speaking before they write them down. For example, a group discussion on climate change could generate ideas for an essay; or a role play on a public meeting about plans for a new stadium could provide ideas for 'Letters to the Editor'.

Sample lesson 16 contains two 'stimulus' activities: one based on listening to a story, and the other based on realia.

b Working together

Cooperative writing where learners brainstorm ideas together, or write in pairs or groups, can also help to generate ideas on the principle that sharing an idea can help to generate more ideas (two heads are better than one!). Sample lesson 16 uses cooperative writing to help learners to get ideas.

c Interactive writing activities

We can help learners with the questions of *Why am I writing?* and *Who am I writing to?* by using interactive writing activities, where the learners write letters which are then 'delivered' by the teacher to another learner, who writes a reply. You can then use the texts the learners have written as a reading task. Making the writing activity into a game like this gives the learners a sense of audience and a purpose. Sample lesson 16 uses interactive writing in the final 'free' writing stage of the lesson.

Writing lessons can contain all three types of writing task, in a progression from accuracy work through guided writing to free writing, or they may simply focus on guided writing or free writing.

Process writing

Another way of helping learners to express their ideas and organize them logically is through **process writing**. This means dividing the writing activity into several stages, each of which practises a sub-skill important in the writing process, for example:

- brainstorm ideas about what to write
- choose ideas and group them under headings
- order the ideas and plan the structure, for example, introduction, arguments for, arguments against, conclusion
- write rough notes to expand each idea
- write a rough version or draft
- pass it to another learner for feedback
- edit — read through, rewrite, and correct.

Sample lesson 16 is an example of a process writing lesson.

Correction and feedback

Looking at learners' written work gives you a good opportunity to assess their progress and to give them helpful feedback on their errors. But be careful how you correct: it can be very discouraging to a learner when a piece of work come back covered in red ink. You will have to decide which errors are the most important, and mark these only. It is also valuable to the learner to have to think out what the mistake was and correct it him/herself. For these reasons it is useful to have a **correction code**. Underline the place where the error occurs and put a note or symbol in the margin saying what kind of error it is, for example, a mistake in verb tense, or a spelling mistake. Some commonly used symbols in correction codes are:

T   tense
Pr   preposition
S   spelling
WO   word order
WF   word form (for example, using a noun instead of a verb, as in '*we have to analysis this')
WW   wrong word or expression
A   article
Ag   agreement (for example, subject and verb do not agree, as in '*he go to town')
P   punctuation
/   missing word

The stages of a writing lesson

Before   **Lead-in**: In this stage it is important to stimulate the learners' interest and provide them with ideas. You can do this by beginning with a short listening or reading text or discussion on the topic they are going to write about, or in the case of imaginative writing, beginning with a stimulus like pictures, music, or realia.

Language focus: You may like to focus on some structures, vocabulary, or linking words that will be useful to the learners as they write. If you have used a listening or reading text in the lead-in, you can take examples from this. If you are using a model text in a genre-based lesson, you can point out the way it is structured and elicit some useful language. If you are doing process writing you might like to do the language focus later in the lesson, perhaps after the learners have done the first draft.

During	**Writing task**: Set the writing task or tasks. You may be doing a series of tasks, starting with accuracy exercises and progressing through guided to free writing, or you may be doing a series of sub-skills tasks in a process writing lesson. Circulate while the learners are writing to offer help and check their work.
After	**Transfer**: You can use the texts that learners have written as reading texts for other learners to read, with a simple comprehension task. **Language focus**: Take in learners' texts and correct them using a correction code as above.

Selecting writing tasks

The writing activities you choose should

be interesting and motivating
Learners will obviously be more motivated and have more ideas if the task engages their interest or seems relevant to their lives.

be appropriate to the learners' level
Beginners and elementary learners will be able to write texts such as short passages about themselves, simple descriptions of people, an account of their daily routines, etc. As learners progress you can add a range of writing tasks: from simple stories, different types of letters, diaries, newspaper articles, adverts, simple poems, dialogues and plays, through to formal essays and reports.

be appropriate for the kind of learners you are teaching
Some groups of learners may need or prefer different kinds of writing. Young learners will enjoy writing simple stories. A group of newly arrived migrants will need writing related to their everyday lives: form-filling, job applications, CVs, etc. Some groups may have specialized interests: a group of businessmen, for example, will need to learn to write business letters, emails, and reports, students preparing to study abroad will need to practise academic essays. If you have a general group then you can provide a range and variety of kinds of writing, including imaginative and creative writing, like stories and poems, as well as more 'real life' writing, like letters and emails. Imaginative writing can be a lot of fun for learners and the sense of satisfaction and pride and creative 'buzz' that comes from writing a simple story or poem in English will increase learners' confidence and self-esteem.

Sample lessons: focus on writing

	Sample lesson 15	**Sample lesson 16**
Type of activity	Genre-based writing: guided for accuracy	Process writing: free
Lead-in	Using learners' experience of present-giving to talk around the topic	Using realia to introduce the idea of an object having a 'history'
Stimulus	Reading: short notes and thank you letters	Listening to a story, lucky dip, bag of realia
Task	Write a short message and a thank you letter	Writing a story
Language focus	Letter writing conventions Structure of a thank you letter *will*	Linking words for narrative Past passives
Transfer	Learners' letters and replies become a 'Read and complete' task	Learners' stories become a 'Listen and guess' task

3.5 Sample lesson 15

LEVEL	Lower intermediate
SKILLS FOCUS	Writing short messages and thank you letters
	Greetings and offering gifts for different occasions
LANGUAGE	Letter writing conventions
ASSUMED KNOWLEDGE	*Will + infinitive* for predictions
RESOURCES	Writing practice poster, reading texts, flashcards
PREPARATION	Make copies of the reading texts in Stage 2 for each learner (either handouts or a poster copy, see Lesson materials appendix, page 160).
	Prepare flashcards of book, vase, rollerblades, money, and socks in Stage 2.
	Prepare writing practice poster in Stage 5 (see Lesson materials appendix, page …).
TIME GUIDE	40 minutes

Lead-in **1** Ask the class about when they give presents in their countries. Ask about the last time they got a present. *What was it?*

Pre-teach vocabulary **2** Put up the picture flashcards. Explain that these are presents. Check learners know the words for the objects.

Put up the letters from p160 on the board or give them out to the learners. Ask them to look at the pictures and read the texts to answer the question:

Who gave what to whom?
(Answers: 1D, 2C, 3A, 4B, 5E)

> **Comment**
> This sort of matching activity gives a purpose to reading and makes reading the texts more enjoyable and motivating than just reading the letters together with their replies.

Language focus

3 Get learners to check their answers in pairs, then go through the answers with the class. Explain any unfamiliar vocabulary, for example, *congratulations, cheerful*, and *housewarming*.

4 Look at the letters and replies again with the learners. Ask them to identify the greetings in the 'giving' letters:

Happy Birthday
Happy Christmas
Congratulations

Help them to notice the structure of the letters:

1 Greeting	Congratulations
2 Say something about why you chose the gift	I hope this will be useful at university
3 Closing	love from Uncle Peter

Do the same for the thank you letters:

1 Greeting	Dear Uncle Peter
2 Say thank you	Thank you for the money!
3 Say something nice about the gift	What a nice surprise! … It will be very useful
4 Closing	love, Matt

> **Comment**
> Giving the learners the basic structure of a text means that they can use the structure again with different content when they write their own letters.

Writing task: accuracy

5 Put up the writing practice poster. Get learners to fill the blanks with suitable words and to put the sentences in the right order to make the letter. Get learners to check their answers in pairs and then go through with the class.

3.5 Focus on writing

**Writing task:
guided writing**

6 Ask each learner to write their name on a slip of paper. Collect them in and give them out randomly, making sure no one gets their own name. Tell the learners to look at the name they have been given. They should imagine they are giving a present to that person. They should try to choose something suitable for that person and write a short message on a piece of paper, using the structure in Stage 4 as a guide.

> **Comment**
> While learners are writing you can circulate to give help where needed and also to point out errors and help with correcting them.

7 Collect up the notes and give them out again to the person they are addressed to.

That person should write a thank you note to the giver on a different piece of paper.

> **Comment**
> This 'interactive writing' task gives learners a concrete task and a sense of audience. They are writing to someone they know, with a real purpose in mind. These two things make the act of writing much easier. It is an activity which should be a lot of fun and generate warm positive feelings in your class!

Transfer

8 Pin the notes and 'Thank yous' around the class. Ask learners to take a page and write the following column headings across the top:

Present   To   From   Reason for gift   Comment on present

Ask learners to take the page and a pencil and walk around the class to find out who gave what to whom, why they chose that gift, and how the recipient felt. Get them to make notes on the answers. Read out a pair of letters and demonstrate how you would fill in the columns on the board.

Present	To	From	Reason for gift	Comment on present
woollen scarf	Kyoko	Fatima	She always looks cold!	Kyoko says *it's very warm and nice!*

When they have gone around for ten minutes or so, get them to form groups of four or five and sit down to compare their answers. Circulate while they are doing this to monitor the discussion.

> **Comment**
> A completed writing task can become a reading text for other learners.
> This helps to reinforce the language and skills learnt in the lesson.

9 Collect in the notes and thank you letters and correct them using an error correction code.

3.5 Sample lesson 16

LEVEL	Intermediate
SKILLS FOCUS	Telling a story
LANGUAGE	Sequencing events, active and passive verbs
ASSUMED KNOWLEDGE	Past tenses, passives
RESOURCES	Bag, objects, text of story
PREPARATION	Bring in the following objects: doll, book, pencil, paintbrush. Bring a cloth or opaque plastic bag with a selection of small objects, for example, key, ring, photo frame, dice, lacy handkerchief, paperclip, yellow ribbon, toy, small mirror, coin, shell
	Bring in one object that is special to you in some way. Copy the text of the story in Stage 2 (see Lesson materials appendix page 162) or put it on a poster to put up in class. Prepare telling the story. (You can use notes to tell the story or the full text.)
TIME GUIDE	40 minutes

Lead-in

1 Show the class your special object and tell them briefly about its 'history' and why it is special to you. Ask them to think of an object that is special to them in some way and to tell their partner about it. Ask a few individual students to tell the class about the object and why it is special.

> **Comment**
> This part of the lead-in should be kept brief. Its purpose is to introduce the idea of objects having 'histories' and to make this meaningful to the learners by getting them to relate it to their own lives.

2 Put the doll, book, pencil, and paintbrush on the table at the front where everyone can see them. Tell the learners you are going to tell them the life story of one of the objects. They have to guess which object is telling the story. Tell the story (see page 162) as naturally as possible and at the end ask them to guess the object (a pencil).

When they have guessed, tell the story again and ask them to listen for the order of events. You can put them on the board in muddled order to help them, for example:

floated down a river	taken to a shop
taken to a factory	lay on a shelf
cut down	bought by a child
chopped up	taken home
grew in the forest	drew a picture

Get them to number the events in order. Let them check in pairs, then go through numbering the events in order on the board. Finally, put up the poster, or give out copies of the story and let them read it.

> **Comment**
> This 'autobiography' will act as a model for the learners to write their own texts: acting as a general stimulus to give them ideas of what to write and providing more specific examples of the kind of language used in an autobiography. You could deal with this language at this point, but it is more motivating for the learners to move from the stimulus of hearing the story directly into creating their own stories. In this lesson the Language focus element fits better into one of the later stages when the learners are redrafting and working to improve the language of their stories.

Writing task: brainstorming

3 Put learners into groups of 4–6. Pass around the bag of objects. Let each group reach into the bag and take an object. They may all look at it but should keep it hidden from the other groups. Ask them to imagine the history of the object. Get everyone in the group to write one or two sentences about an event in the object's life. They should write as if they were the object, in the same way as the pencil story. When they have finished, get them to share their sentences with the rest of the group.

> **Comment**
> This writing task combines a number of different ways of helping the learners write. As we have seen, it provides a stimulus and a model text for writing. The object they take from the lucky dip bag is another stimulus, providing them with something concrete to write about. As they write they know that they will have to read their story for others to guess and this gives a sense of purpose and audience. The writing is done in a group, which means everyone can put their heads together to think of ideas. Finally the process writing structure of the lesson gives them a chance to draft and redraft: selecting, adding, and expanding ideas, putting them in order and improving and refining the way they are expressed.

Selecting ideas

4 The group should choose whether to keep all the ideas or select some.

Sequencing ideas

5 Together they should decide on the order that the events happened in the object's life story.

Adding ideas

6 They can add events and expand ideas, adding more detail at this point.

3.5 Focus on writing

Language focus

7 At this stage, get students to read the pencil story again to look more closely at the language. Ask, *How many tenses are used? What are they?* Get them to highlight the tenses with a colour code (for example, red for simple past, green for past passive, blue for simple present) on their copies or on the poster. Read the two sentences *I was cut down* and *A child ... bought me.* Why is the active used in one and the passive in the other? Elicit or explain that we use the passive when it is not important who did the action. Then ask them to circle the time expressions and words or phrases that tell you when something happens (for example, *then, next, later*, etc.). They should identify:

a long time ago	one day	for several months	then
later	when (we got there)	now	long ago

Put these up on the board and ask them to brainstorm any other words they know that tell you about time in a story and add these to the board. Point out to them that it is not every event in a story that needs a time word to introduce it. It can make a story sound very clumsy if every sentence begins with *Then* or *Next* or *Later.* In general we use time expressions when we need to make it very clear that one event happened before or after another, or show how much time passed between two events.

> **Comment**
> When the groups have the skeleton of their story, it is time to work more closely on the language. This means going back to the original text to find useful examples of how language is used.

Linking ideas

8 Split the groups into pairs or threes for this stage. Get them to work on exactly how to tell the story, adding in time expressions to make the meaning clear if necessary and checking use of different tenses and active/passive verbs.

Comparing

9 Put the pairs and threes back into their original large groups. Get them to compare versions and choose the best, or combine the best features of the two stories.

> **Comment**
> Splitting the groups up into smaller groups and then bringing them back together means that they will have two versions of the same story to compare. It is easier to evaluate someone else's work than your own and the pairs will learn a lot from each other as they correct errors and choose the best way of expressing ideas.

Finalizing

10 Finally, can they add, delete, or change anything to make the story read better?

Transfer

11 When the groups have finished, get them each to tell their story without saying what the object is. The other groups should guess the object. Collect in the stories and correct them using a correction code or if you have time, type or write them up in a corrected version. Hand them back to the learners getting them to notice the difference between their version and the corrected one. These corrected versions can be used to make a wall display.

4 Putting it together: planning, review, and classroom management

4.1 Planning lessons and lesson sequences

Planning a lesson

When you are planning a lesson, ask these two basic questions:

- What am I going to teach?
- How am I going to teach it?

What am I going to teach: writing a planning outline

You have seen several examples of lesson plans now, together with comments on each stage. The basic framework of the lessons in this book will make a good basis for planning your own lessons. For all lessons it is useful to begin your planning outline with your **aims** (what you want to achieve in the lesson) and your **target language/ skills** (the language or skills you are going to teach).

On page 135 is the planning outline with notes that the teacher might have prepared for 'Asking for directions' in Unit 2.1.

How am I going to teach: procedure

The second part of your plan is called the procedure. This is where you list the stages of your lesson and say what you will do in each stage.

For language lessons the stages will be made up of these stages:

- lead-in (engage attention and create a context)
- introduce the language
- language focus
- check comprehension
- practise the language
- use the language
- feedback
- consolidation.

As we have seen, these can be arranged in different ways to give either a PPP lesson or a Test–teach–test lesson.

For skills lessons, these will be the stages:

- *Before*: Lead-in
             Language focus
- *During*: Task or tasks
- *After*:   Language focus
             Transfer

Include the level and name of your class here

Define the main aim here. This is defined in terms of what you want to achieve in the lesson and what you want your learners to be able to do, for example: by the end of the lesson, learners will be able to ask for and give simple directions

Specify the new language or skills you are going to teach. It helps to list the target language

Try to think about any problems or difficulties that learners may have …

… and try to be prepared with a possible solution

Keep within the time limits of the lesson

Class
Class 1 Elementary

Aims
To introduce and practise language giving directions
To revise vocabulary for town places
- To revise *Where* and *How* questions
- To revise prepositions of place
- To introduce imperatives and vocabulary for giving directions

Personal aim
Less TTT and more STT!

Target language/skills
How do I get to …
Turn left /right at the …
Take the … on the left/right
Go straight on

Assumed knowledge
present simple, present continuous, *going to*, *yes/no* and *Wh-* questions
Town places
Opposite, next to

Anticipated problems
Learners may have forgotten vocabulary for town places

Solution
Use flashcards to revise places

Materials
Flashcards
Taped dialogue + transcript
Board (substitution table)
Information gap cards

Time guide
50 minutes

Your main aim can be broken into secondary or subsidiary aims

You can also have a personal aim. This is something you want to improve about your teaching, for example: less TTT (teacher talking time)

Write here language that you expect them to know already

List all the materials that you will use during the lesson

Figure 4.1 *Planning outline for a lesson*

As you begin teaching it will help you to make detailed procedural plans. As you get more experienced you will be able to simplify and shorten this process, but at the beginning it will help you focus and think out exactly what you need to do. Details to include are:

- name of stage
- aims for each stage
- interaction *
- procedure (what you will do in each stage)
- materials you will need
- timing for each stage.

For more on interaction, see 'Classroom interaction' page 146.

You can experiment with different ways of laying this information out, until you find one that seems clearest to you. Here is an example of how the teacher might write a procedure for the first few stages of the lesson on 'Asking for directions':

Stage	Aim	Interaction	Procedure	Materials	Timing
1 Lead-in	1 To get the students interested and predicting the content of the dialogue 2 To create a context	T–Ss	Show flashcard of lost tourist Get students to discuss situation and predict what is going to happen	Flashcard	2 minutes
2 Introduce the language	To set up a situation to introduce the new language meaningfully in context	T–Ss	Play taped dialogue with focus question to establish situation. Play again with task: students trace route on map. Play again with transcript	Cassette tape and recorder Map	10 minutes
3 Check comprehension	1 To check how much of the new language learners understood 2 To explain meaning of new words	T–Ss Ss–T	Ask comprehension questions Draw map on the board and go through the route	Board	5 minutes
4 Language focus	To explain form, meaning, and use of new words	T–Ss	Put up board diagrams of the directions Put new language up with substitution table	Board	5 minutes
5 Practise the language 1	To give students controlled practice in using the target language	T–Ss	Substitution drill with Flashcards	Flashcards	5 minutes
6 Practise the language 2	To give students controlled practice in using the language	Ss–Ss	Label desks with names of places. One student is a tourist and asks the way, the others direct him/her. He/she follows directions	Students labels desks	10 minutes

Figure 4.3 *Procedural lesson plan*

What makes a good plan?

When you have written your plan, look at it critically.

Here is a list of questions you can ask yourself:

- Is the aim realistic and appropriate for your students?
- Is the target language the right level? Is there the right amount?
- Are the stages of the lesson in a logical order?
- Have you predicted what might go wrong and developed a good plan to deal with it?
- Is your timing realistic?
- Are your materials attractive and interesting?
- Are the activities varied, realistic, and appropriate to the level of your learners?
- Is there a balance of T–S and S–S interaction?

How to plan a sequence of lessons

Each lesson in your sequence must lead on from the one before in a series of small steps — just like the stages in a lesson. There should be a balance of skills throughout your sequence and a variety of activities. The sequence should be well paced so that enough time is given to activities, but not so that they are allowed to go on so long that they become boring. Finally, there should be time allocated for feedback, review, and remedial work.

What a sequence of lessons might look like

Here is an example of a scheme of work for an Intermediate level class. A **scheme of work** outlines the content and main aims of each lesson in a given period. It gives an idea of what the lesson will contain and how it fits in and builds on other lessons. The teacher can then write a more detailed lesson plan for each lesson.

This scheme of work is based on a course book unit on the topic 'Crime'. For the morning lessons, the teacher uses the course book as a basis and adds in some related speaking activities and some extra grammar exercises. In the afternoons, she does a series of **integrated skills** activities (activities which combine a variety of the language skills) using extra materials.

137

Week 5:	Coursebook Unit 5
Topic:	crime
Grammar: revision:	past tenses; new: past passives
Lexical area:	crime vocabulary
Functions:	reporting events, giving opinions
Skills focus:	students read and listen to a variety of news articles and interviews on crime and practise writing and role playing their own news items—leading up to making a television news programme on the last day

	MORNINGS course book: language work	AFTERNOONS supplementary material: skills work
Monday	Starter: Alibi game Unit 5: p. 25 Grammar revision on past simple/past continuous/past perfect	Extract from radio news on burglaries Students role play interview using info from broadcast
Tuesday	Unit 5 p. 26 Role play: Solve the crime Grammar: introduce past passives	Give students selection of newspaper headlines: in groups they write news stories to go with them
Wednesday	Leave out Unit 5 p. 27 (too hard!) Replace with: pyramid discussion: Crime and punishment Grammar: past passives	Jigsaw reading: Crimes that went wrong. Students interview each other to find out stories
Thursday	Game: It wasn't me officer! Unit 5 p. 28; Ex. 9 adapt discussion so students talk about their own countries) Grammar: mixed tenses; active and passive	Eyewitness stories Students listen and then write up as article
Friday	Unit 5 p. 29 (review) Test on passives and mixed tenses	Students use different newspaper articles on crime to create a television news programme

Figure 4.3 *Scheme of work*

Comments

Notice how

- The language work and skills are organized under a single topic.
- To adapt a course book to the needs of your class, you may need to leave out, replace, or adapt some activities and add others. In the scheme of work above, the teacher has omitted one section she feels to be unsuitable for her students' level and replaced it with another activity (Wednesday morning); and has adapted another activity to give it a more personal focus for her particular students (Thursday morning).
- The skills work in the afternoons uses and extends vocabulary and grammatical structures taught in the morning.
- All the afternoon activities are preparation for the final task of the week (making their own news programme).
- Activities are varied. For example, there are different types of speaking tasks (games, role play, discussion, and interview).
- There is a balance of skills (listening, reading, speaking, and writing).
- The week ends with a review and a short test, which will give the teacher feedback on whether the class have mastered the language or whether they will need review and further practice.

  If you have access to different course books, skills books, grammar workbooks, and teachers' resource books, you can use these as sources of supplementary activities for a scheme of work like the one above. For a list of recommended books, please see Further reading. If you have access to radio, television, internet, or newspapers in English, these **authentic materials** are also a good source of supplementary reading and listening texts, especially if you have a higher level group. At lower levels, you will have to be careful about the level of the language in the authentic material you find and be sure it is not so difficult that it will discourage your students. If you do not have access to extra published or authentic materials, you can use or adapt ideas like the ones in this book and the other books in this series to create your own 'home-made' materials.

4.2 Review, assessment, and remedial work

In the lessons we have looked at in this book there has been a 'production–feedback–error correction' cycle within each lesson. It is important to build this cycle into a sequence of lessons too.

Review

Begin a lesson with a quick review of what the students learnt in the last lesson. Try to make the review an enjoyable activity. Here are some ideas:

- Do a short oral practice activity (T–S or S–S).
- Play a game: 'Find someone who …' is an enjoyable game that can be adapted to practise a range of structures, for example: 'How many … have you got?' Before starting the game, it is a good idea to elicit the first couple of questions that the students will need.

Find someone who:	Write the name
has got three brothers	_____
has got two aunts	_____
has got one sister	_____
has got four uncles	_____

- Unscrambling: give learners jumbled sentences to sort out, for example, 'is your name What?' For higher level classes, you could give the students a short text with the sentences in muddled order.
- Matching: learners have cards with either a question or an answer on it, and they have to go round the class to find the person who has the right answer/question.
- Competition: put learners in groups to see how many words they can remember from the vocabulary in the previous lesson.

You can also begin a week with a review of the previous week's work, to refresh learners' minds after the weekend.

Assessment

Assessment is a complex area. This is a brief introduction to give you an overview of different types of test and their uses, together with a few examples of test formats.

Reasons for testing

You can assess students' performance for different reasons:

- To find out their level and put them in an appropriate class with students of a similar level at the beginning of their course. This is called a **placement test**.
- To find out how well a student can use the language. These tests are often national or international exams with the award of a certificate if students pass. These exams are called **proficiency tests**.
- To find out what gaps there are in a student's knowledge of the language so that you can tailor your teaching to address their needs. This is called a **diagnostic test**.
- (At the end of a course) To see how much the students have retained. This is called an **achievement test**.
- (During a course) To check on how well students have mastered what you have taught them and identify what the main problems are in order to plan remedial work if necessary. These are called **progress tests**. This is probably the type of test you will be using most often. You will probably plan them in on your scheme of work, weekly, fortnightly, or monthly.

You can also check students' progress informally by monitoring their performance during tasks, marking their written work, and checking their answers to reading and listening tasks.

Assessing for placement of students

4.2 Review, assessment, and remedial work

Types of test

You can use tests like gap fill, multiple choice, and true/false questions to test learners' accuracy. These can be used to test grammar items, pronunciation, vocabulary items, and comprehension in receptive skills (listening and reading). Tests like this, that only test one thing at a time, are called **discrete item tests**. They are objective, meaning they do not depend on someone's judgement, because there is only one right answer. You can grade them easily with a number or a percentage.

However the productive skills (speaking and writing) cannot be tested by objective discrete item tests, because they are about meaningful communication. Speaking is best tested by in interview, a role play, or other speaking tasks such as 'describe a picture' performed with the teacher or in pairs. The teacher (or an examiner) can then grade the students' performance. Writing is best tested by a writing task such as writing a story about a sequence of pictures, writing an opinion essay, or writing a reply to a letter/email. These tests are called **integrative tests** because they test a number of things at the same time: vocabulary, collocation, and many grammar points, as well as pronunciation and fluency in the case of speaking tasks. They are more subjective than the discrete item tests: the examiner's judgement is needed to decide whether a student's performance is good or bad.

Establishing grading criteria

You can establish criteria to make grading less subjective by trying to define exactly what each grade means in terms of what the learner can do with the language. Overleaf is an example of 'Can do' statements used as grading criteria, from the Council of Europe's Common European Framework CEF assessment criteria.

What makes a good test?

The tests you give should be valid and reliable. 'Valid' means that the test should test only what it claims to measure:

1 Discrete item tests should test only language that the learners have learnt in the course. If you have taught learners the simple past but not the other past tenses for example, it is not a valid test to include items which test the past continuous or the present perfect.

2 You should test in a similar way to the way you teach. If you have been teaching communicatively then your test should include activities and tasks where the learners have to use language communicatively, for example, taking part in a role play or conversation.

Proficient user	C2	Can easily understand virtually everything heard or read. Can summarize information from different sources, reconstructing arguments. Can express him/herself spontaneously, very fluently and precisely, using finer shades of meaning even in more complex situations.
	C1	Can understand a wide range of difficult, longer texts. Can express him/herself fluently and spontaneously without much searching for expressions. Can use language flexibly and effectively for social, academic, and professional purposes. Can produce clear, well-structured, detailed text on complex subjects.
Independent user	B2	Can understand the main ideas of complex text, including technical discussions in his/her field. Can interact with native speakers without major difficulties. Can produce clear, detailed text on a wide range of subjects.
	B1	Can understand the main points of familiar matters in different topics such as work, school, leisure, etc. Can deal with most situations while travelling. Can produce simple connected text on familiar topics.
Basic user	A2	Can understand basic sentences and frequently used expressions Can communicate with simplicity on familiar topics. Can describe his/her background.
	A1	Can understand and use familiar everyday expressions and very basic phrases. Can introduce him/herself and others and can ask about personal details, such as where he/she lives, people he/she knows, and things he/she has.

Figure 4.4 *CEF assessment criteria*

In general, the tests you give your students should be a combination of discrete item tests, which test language knowledge and understanding, and integrative tests, which test ability to communicate.

'Reliable' means that the test should give results you can trust. This means that instructions should be clear and easy to understand, there should be no mistakes in the presentation of the test, and that the conditions should be the same for all candidates.

Planning remedial work

Students have a lot to remember when they are learning a language, and cannot always use or remember what they have been taught. If students are making lots of mistakes with something you have taught them, you will need to give them remedial work, where you re-teach the target language in a new way, and give the students practice exercises and activities or self study materials.

You are most likely to integrate remedial work on the basis of progress test performance. If you find that there are errors that the whole class, or most of the class, are making, it makes sense to take a lesson or part of a lesson to re-teach and explain the structure and give the class activities and exercises to help them.

When marking tests, you may also find errors that only one or only a couple of students are making. In this case you may like to give an individual exercise to the student(s) involved, or refer them to activities in self study grammar practice books such as *Oxford Practice Grammar*.

You will also find instances when it is appropriate to give individuals immediate feedback on their writing—again, referring them to self study grammar practice books—or after a speaking activity. There are several ways you can deal with errors that you hear in a speaking activity, and these are dealt with under 'error correction' in the next section (page 151).

When you are planning your scheme of work it makes sense to allow time for whole class remedial work.

4.3 Classroom management

In this section we will look at:

- classroom layout
- classroom interaction
- roles of the teacher
- classroom language
- error correction and feedback
- dealing with diversity.

Classroom layout

Depending on what activities you are doing, you will need to arrange the objects in your classroom — the desks, chairs, and other items. Here are some questions you can ask yourself as you set up the classroom:

- Can everyone see me?
- Can everyone see the board?
- Can the learners talk to each other?
- Can they hear the tape recorder?

Here are some options for arranging the desks:

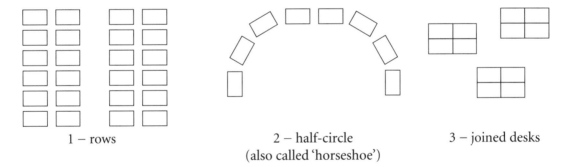

1 – rows   2 – half-circle (also called 'horseshoe')   3 – joined desks

Figure 4.5 *Options for desk arranging*

1 Rows

If this is your classroom layout, you can easily organize group and pair work by getting learners to work with the person next to them, or by getting pairs to turn their chairs so they work with the pair behind them.

2 Half-circle ('horseshoe')

This is a common layout in private language schools or state tertiary institutions with smaller classes. The teacher is the focus of attention but the learners can also interact with each other across the half-circle. It provides space for the learners to meet in the middle to act out a drama or role play for the rest of the class. It also means that the learners can see and have easy access to the board.

3 Joined desks

This is a good layout for classes that do a lot of project work or **group work**. It gives them lots of space for materials and for groups of 4–6 learners to work together. It allows the teacher to spend time with each group and for the learners to interact with the teacher. It is less teacher-focused than the other two patterns.

Other options are for the desks to be moved to the side of the class to provide space for activities such as mingling activities (like 'Find someone who ... ') or action activities (like 'Listen and do').

Classroom interaction

Let's now look at possible patterns of interaction in the classroom.

Teacher to students (T→Ss)

This **interaction pattern** is common at the beginning of class or an activity, when the teacher is eliciting, explaining, or giving instructions. Be careful, as this interaction pattern involves a lot of **TTT** (teacher talking time), and you need to make sure that there is lots of time for STT (student talking time).

Teacher to students (T→Ss) and student(s) to teacher (Ss→T)

Sometimes it is appropriate for learners to interact with the teacher either individually or as a whole class in a 'question and answer' activity or in a drill. Asking students to respond individually gives you the chance to see how individual learners are doing but some may find it threatening to be 'put on the spot' (asked to talk without any warning).

Half class to half class (Ss→Ss)

In some practice or review activities you can divide the class in half and the two half-class groups interact with each other in dialogue practice, a team game, or a guessing game. These activities give everyone the chance to contribute and they can be a lot of fun.

Student to class (S→Ss)

After the class has been working in groups, one learner from each group can 'report back' to the rest of the class. This is a valuable interaction, as it brings the class together again after group work and rounds the activity off.

Student to student (open pairs) (S—▸S)

Sometimes you will have one student interact with another, with the rest of the class listening. This allows you to listen in and give immediate feedback, and is useful when you are checking learner comprehension.

Student to student (S—▸S)

In many activities the learners work together in pairs or small groups, and in some activities they walk around the class talking to other learners at random, in a 'mingling' activity. This student-to-student interaction pattern is the most valuable for giving learners speaking practice. It are also valuable for you, as it gives you the opportunity to listen to your learners and get feedback on how well they understand and are able to use the language you have taught them.

Pair and group work can be frustrating for some learners who believe that the best way to learn is from a native speaker, and that speaking to other non-native speakers (learners whose first language is not English) is a waste of time. It can help if you explain how much more speaking practice they are getting in pairs or groups than in T–S interaction, and if you monitor very carefully and provide feedback that helps the learners to correct their mistakes. It also helps if you move the learners around so that no one is 'stuck' with someone for very long.

One way of making sure learners talk to a variety of other learners is by using mingling activities. These have the added benefit of giving the learners the choice of who to talk to and for how long, which is more like communication in the real world outside the classroom. Mingling activities also give learners the opportunity to develop interactive skills in English (starting an interaction, developing the conversation, and finishing the interaction).

Individual work (S)

Learners do not have to interact with each other all the time: a little mental space can be welcome in a busy lesson! Learners may work individually on writing activities or they may need individual planning time before a speaking activity.

In any lesson it is important to consider which interaction patterns best fit your aim for that activity. It is also important to vary interaction patterns to maintain pace and interest

Roles of the teacher

In the classroom you will play two main roles: information giver and facilitator. Within these two categories there are several sub-categories, for example:

Teacher as information giver

Explainer
You will have to explain various things to your class such as how to play a game or do a grammar exercise. You may also have to explain grammar, or the meaning of words that the students do not know. Particularly with lower levels you will often use mime, action, pictures, tables, and diagrams.

Demonstrator
You will have to demonstrate some things to the class through actions — for example, by miming 'jump' to show them what the word means or by showing through your own actions how a game is played.

Organizer and instruction giver
You will have to give instructions to the class such as, *Now get into groups of four* or *Turn to page 24.*

Controller
Depending on the group, you may have to restore order from time to time, for example by reminding the class to speak English, asking them to speak more quietly, or preventing more dominant learners from interrupting others.

Route planner
In this role you may give your students a sense of direction by outlining what you will cover in the course or in a lesson.

Teacher as facilitator

Guide
Instead of explaining and giving information you can elicit information from your learners, remodelling where necessary, so that they formulate their own explanations of grammar or vocabulary items.

Monitor
In this role you will be listening to your students when they are speaking to each other in pairs or groups, noting errors to discuss with them later.

Support system
Again when students are working by themselves or in groups, your role is to circulate to give help and provide language when asked.

Feedback giver
In this role you give students feedback on their performance by correcting their errors – or better encouraging them to identify and correct their own errors if they can.

Counsellor
In this role you will give students advice and support on things they can do to help themselves learn, for example, on ways of learning vocabulary at home.

Classroom language

Giving instructions

It is important to be very clear about how you want the students to work and to give your instructions clearly and simply:

- Break your instructions down: 'one step, one sentence' is a good rule.
- Wait for the students to carry out that step before going on to the next one.
- Demonstrate what to do: actions are often clearer than words.

So, for example, if you say the following, your learners are likely to feel very confused:

Now I want you to get into threes and fours, take the pack of cards I give you and deal them out to everyone One student begins by selecting a picture card and asking a question, for example: Do you like ice cream or Do you play tennis? The player with the matching card puts it down and answers the question.

They will find it much easier to understand if you break the instructions down like this:

T   *Now get into groups: you four work together, you four work together ...* (waits for the students to get into groups, checks they are all settled).

     I'm going to give you a pack of cards (gives them out).

     Everyone got a pack of cards? OK, deal them out like this (demonstrates and waits for the class to follow).

     Have you all done that? Good. Now watch me (goes over to one group and takes one player's hand of cards).

Player 1 takes a card. Any card (takes a card) *and puts it on the table* (puts card on the table).

Then ask a question … This card (shows them the card) *is a picture of ice cream. So … What can I say?*

ss: *Do you like ice cream? Do you want ice cream? Do you eat ice cream? Can you buy me an ice cream?*

t: *Yes! All of those questions are OK. For example* (puts card on table), *Do you like ice cream? Now who has the matching car—who has ice cream too?*

s: *Me!*

t: *OK. Put your ice cream on the table* (mimes) *…* (waits for the student to do this)

Now answer my question: Do you like ice cream?

s: *Yes I do!*

t: *Then it is Player 2's turn* (points to the next student). *You try, Ana.*

ana: (taking picture of tennis racquet) *Ah … Do you play tennis?*

s: with matching picture: *No, I don't. I would like to learn …*

t: *Great! OK everybody? Any problems? Do you all know how to play? All right,—begin!*

At the beginning you will need to think out carefully how you are going to give instructions but this will become easier and more automatic as you go on.

Giving feedback

The teacher's role while group and pair activities are taking place is to monitor, i.e. pay careful attention to how the activity is going. This includes making sure that all the learners know what to do and are actively participating, and also making a note on how successfully the learners are communicating. This then informs the feedback that the teacher gives the learners.

Feedback can simply take the form of saying 'Well done'. It is important to give positive feedback as this boosts the learners' confidence and motivates them for future activities.

Error correction

Feedback can also take the form of correction, which can be done in several ways. It is sometimes best to correct students immediately (as soon as they make the mistake) and sometimes best to wait until after they have finished speaking.

Self-correction

Self-correction is when the learner corrects their own mistake.

Immediate self-correction
As soon as you hear a mistake, you can bring the mistake to the learner's attention. For example, if the learner says *I go shopping yesterday* you can encourage the learner to self-correct by saying, *I* [pause] *shopping yesterday*, or *I go shopping*?, or by asking, *What is the past of 'go'?*. Another option is to use finger correction as in the example lesson in 2.1 (see page 15).

The advantage of immediate self-correction is that the learner is made aware of the mistake and has a chance to use the correct version in practice. However, correcting immediately means that the flow of communication is interrupted while the error is attended to. It can be time-consuming and the learner might not be able to find the answer — which might mean that the learner loses self-confidence or feels embarrassed. However, many students don't mind immediate self-correction, and it should be used sometimes, as it helps the learner think about the language and develop a more autonomous and active approach to their learning.

You will probably use immediate self-correction in a whole-class T–S activity or when going round monitoring learners as they are writing.

Self-correction after the activity
In pair and group work it is best not to interrupt the learners to correct them, as this will interfere with fluency. Instead, you will need to give feedback on errors after the activity. There are many options for doing this as we have seen in the sample lessons. With written activities you can use a correction code (see page 121) or rewrite the text so the learner can compare their version with the correct one (see Sample lesson 16).

With either speaking or writing activities you can write up errors anonymously on the board and ask learners to correct them (see Section 2.1, and Stage 8 of Sample lesson 5). As a variation, you could also mix in correct sentences with the errors and ask the class to identify the correct sentences.

Peer correction

Peer correction is when a student's mistake is corrected by their peers: the other students. Any immediate peer correction will happen spontaneously, while the learners are working together, and you have no control over this. You can, however, set up peer correction for after the activity has finished. One way of doing this is to record learners' errors on slips of paper as you monitor their speaking, and get learners to work in pairs on correcting the errors one slip at a time (see Stages 3 and 6 in Sample lesson 14, pages 114–15). You can do this as a mingling activity, where each student is given a small card with a sentence on it containing one error, and has to ask three different people what they think the error is. Both of these activities will end with the learners writing up the incorrect phrase and correction on the board and discussing it with the class, under your supervision.

One of the most important judgements a teacher has to make is how far the learners and class as a whole have understood and developed the ability to say or do something. Monitoring provides the teacher with data for this judgement. The teacher needs to keep a range of questions in mind. For example, if the lesson has focused on making and responding to invitations, can the learners perform these functions? What sort of mistakes do they make? Are they struggling to use the language fluently enough? Are they pronouncing the phrases accurately enough to be understood? Depending on the answers to these questions, the teacher needs to decide whether the learners need more practice, and if so when. This affects their overall planning, as the next lesson or lessons might need to be rethought to provide more time to get the learners to the point where they can use the language. This process of monitoring, judging, and planning according to the learners' performance is important for the learners' overall progress.

Dealing with diversity

This book ends where it began — with people: their different needs and wants, different levels and abilities, and different personalities and learning styles — and suggests some practical ways of dealing with these diverse demands. It may feel like an impossible task to try to satisfy all the individual needs of your students, and you are right! But there are some practical things you can do to make sure that there is something for everyone in each of your lessons.

Different needs, levels, and abilities

As we saw at the beginning of this book, your students will have different needs and abilities: some may need more speaking practice, others may need more focus on grammatical accuracy. And even when students are put into classes according to level, there will be a range of levels and abilities within any class. There are three things you can do about this:

The first is to make sure you provide a range of activities and a balance of skills. For example, make sure there is both fluency practice for the hesitant speakers and grammar exercises for the fluent but inaccurate students.

The second involves making learners aware of their needs and individual differences. Let them know you are aware of this too and that you will be doing your best to provide a course that has 'something for everyone'. A good way of doing this is to give your class a questionnaire which asks learners to say why they are learning English and what they want to be able to do in English. Ask them to list what they feel is important for them and which areas they need to practise most. Go round helping them and looking at their answers so that you get a feel for what they need, and then ask them to discuss their answers with a partner and then in a group of four. Each group of four can then report back to the class. There may be two different outcomes to this. One is that you find that your class all want roughly the same thing—to be able to speak fluently for example or to be able to read newspapers—in which case this will help you organize your teaching to reflect their needs. The other (more likely!) outcome is that you find that students want very different things out of the course, in which case you can let them know that you will teach a balanced course with 'something for everyone'. In this way students will become aware that there are different needs in the class and that they must balance their needs with those of other students.

A third thing you can do is to provide some opportunities for **autonomous learning** where learners can choose their own tasks. You may be working in a school which has a **self-access centre** where students can go and choose from a range of material to work on by themselves—but you can also build up a mini self-access centre in your own classroom, with activities for 'early finishers' to work on quietly while they wait for the rest of the class to complete an activity. This could include grammar exercises, questions from a quiz, or vocabulary from recent lessons.

Different learning styles: balance and variety

As we saw in the introduction, people learn in different ways. You cannot, of course, offer a range of choices for every activity to suit different learning styles! But you *can* provide a range of different activities in your teaching to appeal to a range of different learning styles. For example:

■ Make sure some of your activities appeal to visual learners (reading, writing, pictures, diagrams), some to auditory learners (songs, listening, repeating, speaking), and some to kinaesthetic learners (drama, movement, card games, mingling activities).
■ Make sure you have a balance of noisy social activities and quiet reflective ones to appeal to interpersonal and intrapersonal learners (extroverts and introverts).
■ Make sure you have some analytic activities (such as grammar explanations and gap fills) balanced with some activities which help learners absorb new language (such as read and retell, listen and discuss, role play, drama, information gap activities, and games which involve repetition of language patterns).
■ Make sure you have some logical exercises, such as puzzles and games, balanced with some more creative tasks, such as poetry writing and drama.
■ Make sure you have some closed tasks with a definite end, such as gap fill and completing a task, balanced with more open ended tasks with no fixed outcome such as role play, drama, and creative writing.
■ Make sure there is a balance of factual subject matter (topics, descriptions, argument, and opinion) with more personal topics (topics dealing with emotions and feelings).
And if sometimes you can offer a choice, for example,

Do this gap fill exercise on the past continuous

OR

Imagine you were waiting at a bus stop when a spaceship landed in the street. Write a story describing what was happening before … and what happened when it landed.

… you will have some happy students!

In two teams, run to the board to match the sentences with the pictures... ...until the music stops!

Different personalities

Your students will also have very different personalities. Depending on the mix of personalities this may produce harmony—or conflict! You may think that this does not have much to do with learning and that it is your job to teach, not make sure they all get on with each other! But in fact research has shown that a cohesive class, where students get on well and enjoy being part of a group, can enhance learning. A cohesive group is also much easier and more pleasant to teach—a much nicer place to be! So it is in everyone's interest to try to promote a supportive and enjoyable group atmosphere. Here are a few simple ideas for promoting a good group feeling:

Have fun! A group that laughs together will be a good group. Tell jokes, bring in funny stories—listen to their jokes …

Keep the seating arrangements flexible: find ways of getting people to change places and work with different partners or different groups. This means that cliques won't develop and it also means that your students' language will develop more: if they always work with the same partner they may get restricted to the same limited language.

Get students to exchange personal information so that they get to know each other well. Think how you can personalize grammar exercises: for example, to practise the present perfect you can use an activity which involves students telling each other about their own life experiences, and to practise the future continuous each student could predict what their partner will be doing in ten years' time.

Get the class to create group 'products': tasks like writing a story together, producing a class magazine, or putting on a short play together will help a class to make friends and will give them a tremendous sense of achievement, which is very motivating.

Keep the atmosphere positive. It is worth starting the week or the lesson with a very simple short activity that is aimed at making people feel good. For example:

- *Think of something nice that happened this morning—it can be as simple as seeing a butterfly or the smell of newly cut grass.*
- *Close your eyes and imagine you are in a very beautiful place … now describe it to your partner.*
- *Make a medal for another student in the class, awarding it for the special qualities they have.*
- *Imagine you have a present for your partner: imagine what the present might be and mime giving it.*

We hope that you have enjoyed this book and have found it useful. We have taught English now in many countries and many different situations, and wherever we have been in the world have always found it to be a challenging, exciting, and invigorating job. We hope that wherever you are teaching now, and wherever you may go, you will enjoy the rich experience of teaching and the fun, laughter, and joy of the teaching–learning relationship as much as we do.

Appendices

Lesson materials

Sample lesson 10

Story outline

Man went surfing.
He was quite far from the beach.
He saw a dark triangle shape on the surface of the sea.
He realized it was a shark.
He panicked and started swimming towards the beach.
He saw more black shapes in the water.
His mind went blank: terrified.
The shapes got closer.
He tried to get on his board.
The shapes formed a circle round the board.
He thought he was going to die.
He fell off the board.
Underwater he saw lots of shapes.
He looked closer and realized they were dolphins.
They surrounded him and led him to the shore.
They had saved him from the shark.

Expanded version

I read this story in the paper the other day—it happened in New Zealand, I think. A man was surfing and he was getting worried because he was quite far out from the land. Anyway, he was surfing when he suddenly saw this triangular black fin coming straight towards him—right at him! Well, he panicked—the fin was huge and coming straight for him—and he knew sharks sometimes attack surfers—it's because they can see the shape of the surfboard and think it's a seal. Anyway, he saw the shark in the water—he was terrified; sick with panic—and started swimming for the shore. Then he saw some dark shapes in the water—he wondered—was it more sharks? He didn't know what to do; his mind went blank; he was paralysed with fear. The shapes got closer and closer. He tried to get on his surfboard ... the shapes got closer and formed a circle round the board. The surfer fell off the board into the water, and the shapes came closer and he thought he was going to die ... then he realized it was a group of dolphins. He was confused and wondered what was going to happen—would the shark chase them instead? Then the dolphins surrounded him—he was in the middle—they surrounded him so the shark couldn't get him and they swam to the shore—they pulled him along with them. At first he was puzzled—he didn't know what was happening—then he was amazed: he couldn't believe it—they led him to shore—he reached the land—the dolphins had saved him from the shark.

Lesson materials

Sample lesson 12

The name game

Identical twins often have astonishing stories. One pair of identical twin boys, born in Ohio, USA, were separated at birth and adopted by different families. Neither of the boys knew about his twin, but there were some amazing coincidences. To begin with, neither family knew the other, but both families called the boys James. At school the boys liked the same subjects and both of them were good at drawing and woodwork. The boys did various jobs but at one point both of the boys wanted to be policemen. Both of them married women called Linda and both of them had sons, one called James Alan and one called James Allan. They were married for several years but in the end both brothers divorced their wives and married again. Here another extraordinary coincidence happened: both new wives were called Betty. The final coincidence in this astonishing story: both men owned dogs—and both dogs were called Toy. For many years, the brothers lived different lives, neither of them knowing about the other, until forty years after the separation the brothers were reunited.

Sample lesson 13

Our City's Problems

Westport is growing fast—too fast some say! The list of problems is growing every day. Most of us live in the suburbs and work in the centre. There is no good rail service so traffic jams are a daily problem for us. Our roads are too crowded and there are far too many accidents. Our services are just not good enough. Our hospital is too small. Our schools are overcrowded. There are not enough policemen. Our city centre has had to grow too quickly and is a jumble of badly built office blocks and apartments. Ask people what they think of Westport. Nine times out of ten you get the same replies, 'It's boring!', 'It's ugly!', 'There's nothing to do!' We all know what this means: unemployment and crime is a growing problem—particularly among young people. But we have a hard question for the City Council: the increase in population means an increase in the money the council gets from taxes. How is the money going to be spent? Come to the public meeting and have your say!

Which do YOU think is most important?

A new hospital	A leisure and sports centre
Better roads	An arts centre
A better railway: more trains	Redeveloping the city centre
New schools	Job creation for young people
More police	

Sample lesson 14

Role play cards   1   CASHIER
You saw the three robbers come into the bank at about 3pm. It happened so quickly you can't remember a lot, but one robber was very tall and one was short. They all wore blue uniform and stockings over their heads and carried guns. You sounded the alarm as soon as they left. You think they took about £200,000 in cash.

2   CUSTOMER
You were in the bank when the three men rushed in. It was about 3pm. They wore blue uniform and stockings over their heads and carried guns. Everyone was screaming. The man nearest you had a tattoo on his arm. He was very tall. You don't remember much about the others.

3   PASSENGER AT BUS STOP
You were waiting at the bus stop near the bank when a white van pulled up and three men in uniform got out. They carried briefcases. You thought they were security guards. The driver of the car waited for them outside the bank. He had dark hair and a big nose. You didn't see them come out again because your bus came. It was a bit before 3 o'clock.

4   PASSER-BY
You were passing the bank when three uniformed men rushed out and jumped into a white van. There was another man inside the van. You thought they were security guards but then, as they drove off you heard people screaming inside the bank, so you quickly looked at the number plate of the van. It was 'ZPD 5023H'.

5   GREEN STREET RESIDENT 1
A white van parked in your street around 3.30. It's a very quiet street and it's not near shops, so strangers don't usually park there. You were annoyed as they parked in your parking space. Three or four men got out. One was tall with a beard, one was short with glasses. You went out to ask them to move but you were very surprised to see them getting into a green car and driving off again.

6   GREEN STREET RESIDENT 2
You were coming back from work and listening to the radio news in your car. It mentioned a bank robbery. The thieves had been seen getting into a white van. You parked and got out of the car and couldn't believe your eyes. In front of you was a white van number ZPD 5023H. You went in and phoned the police immediately. This was about 4 pm.

7   MOTORIST

You were driving along the motorway, about 4 o'clock, in the fast lane when a green car overtook you on the inside and swerved in front of you, going very fast. You took the number (W1789 XNV) because they nearly made you have an accident. They turned off on the airport road and you stopped at the next service station, about 15 minutes later and phoned the police to complain about the driver.

8   AIR PASSENGER

You were trying to park your car at the airport but a green car drove in front of you and took your parking space. You were very annoyed. Four men got out and started to run towards the terminal. One had long hair and a ponytail. You thought they were late for their flight, but later you saw them in the terminal queuing for a flight to Spain.

Police report   Four masked robbers entered the High Street branch of AZQ Bank at around 4pm today. They held up cashiers and customers at gunpoint and escaped with over £100,000 in cash. They were seen getting out of a red van (registration number ZPG 5823H) outside the bank. A witness has said that he hadn't noticed anything unusual: 'They were wearing black uniforms. I thought they were security guard's. The men were seen getting into a white car (registration number W178 LNP) at about 5 o'clock. They were last seen on a quiet country road travelling in the direction of the south coast.

Sample lesson 15

Role play cards

A	B	C	D	E

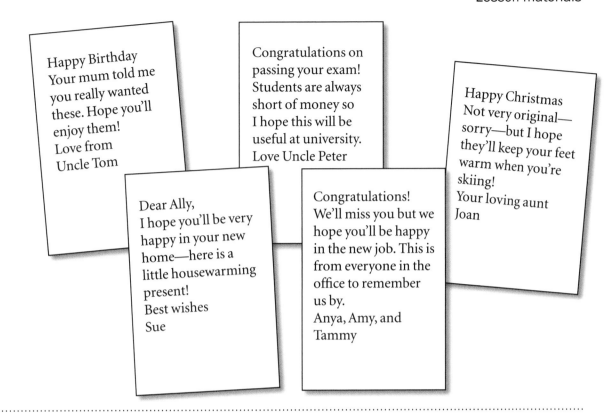

Happy Birthday
Your mum told me you really wanted these. Hope you'll enjoy them!
Love from
Uncle Tom

Congratulations on passing your exam! Students are always short of money so I hope this will be useful at university.
Love Uncle Peter

Happy Christmas
Not very original—sorry—but I hope they'll keep your feet warm when you're skiing!
Your loving aunt
Joan

Dear Ally,
I hope you'll be very happy in your new home—here is a little housewarming present!
Best wishes
Sue

Congratulations!
We'll miss you but we hope you'll be happy in the new job. This is from everyone in the office to remember us by.
Anya, Amy, and Tammy

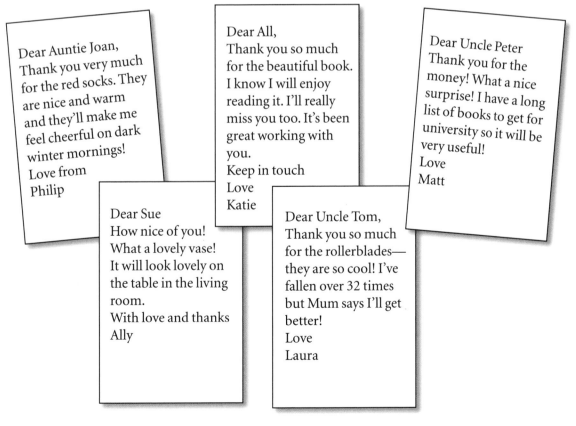

Dear Auntie Joan,
Thank you very much for the red socks. They are nice and warm and they'll make me feel cheerful on dark winter mornings!
Love from
Philip

Dear All,
Thank you so much for the beautiful book. I know I will enjoy reading it. I'll really miss you too. It's been great working with you.
Keep in touch
Love
Katie

Dear Uncle Peter
Thank you for the money! What a nice surprise! I have a long list of books to get for university so it will be very useful!
Love
Matt

Dear Sue
How nice of you! What a lovely vase! It will look lovely on the table in the living room.
With love and thanks
Ally

Dear Uncle Tom,
Thank you so much for the rollerblades—they are so cool! I've fallen over 32 times but Mum says I'll get better!
Love
Laura

Lesson materials

Writing practice poster

Fill in the blanks. Then put the sentences in the right order.

_____ Sally
I _____ it _____ be useful.
I _____ you will be very _____ in your new home!
Here is a little housewarming present
Love _____ Uncle Jo

_____ Uncle Jo
We _____ enjoy using them!
_____ so much for the lovely coffee cups.
_____ from Sally

_____ Tim
I am enclosing some money to say 'Well done!'
_____ on _____ your exam!
I hope you _____ use it to go out and have a good time!
_____ from Auntie May

Dear _____
I _____ use it to go out and celebrate with my friends.
It was very kind of you to send it.
Thank you _____ the money!
Love from _____

Sample lesson 16

Story: notes

Started life as tree in forest—men came with saws and axes—was cut down and sent down river to factory—was chopped up, carved, painted—was taken to shop in city. Lay on a shelf next to cards and writing paper. Child came in and bought me—child took me home, held me in his hand, made something beautiful. Child now a man—I am old now—can't work—I still travel with him—he keeps me for good luck. Child is now famous artist—remember day we drew his first picture.

Story: full text

A long time ago I started life as a tall tree growing in the middle of a deep forest. One day men came with axes and saws. I was cut down and sent floating down a wide river to a factory. There I was chopped up, carved and painted, and then taken with hundreds of others to a shop in a big city. I lay on a shelf for several months next to cards and piles of writing paper. Then one day a child came in with his father. He bought me and took me home. When we got to his room he held me tightly in his hand and together we made something beautiful. Now the child is a man and I am too old to work—but I still travel everywhere with him. He says he keeps me with him for good luck. That child is now a famous artist—and he and I remember that day long ago when we drew his first picture.

Glossary

accuracy	the production of spoken or written language which does not contain errors.	21
achievement test	a test based on the work learners have done during a course.	141
activity	something learners do in order to promote learning, e.g. a speaking activity or a reading comprehension activity.	12
affix	letter(s) added to beginnings or ends of words to change the meaning; e.g. **un**happy, move**ment**. See **prefix**, **suffix**.	46
aim	what the teacher and learners plan to achieve. This can be in a course or in a lesson.	134
assumed knowledge	when planning a lesson, this is the language a teacher assumes the students at this level will already know.	11
antonym	a word that has the opposite meaning to another, e.g. *quick* and *slow*.	47
auditory learning style	learning best when using listening stimuli such as spoken language, music, and sounds.	5
appropriacy	the choosing of language which has the right level of formality for the situation and the relationship between the speakers.	47, 118
authentic material/ authentic texts	a text taken from a real-life source e.g. a newspaper article, or an extract from a TV programme, and used in class without being simplified.	96, 139
autonomous learning	when students take responsibility for their own learning and can use strategies to learn independently outside class.	153
back reference	use of a pronoun to refer back to something or someone already mentioned, e.g. *The girl was unhappy.* **She** *had been waiting for almost half an hour.*	117
choral drill	teacher-led, repetitive, oral practice involving the whole class.	13
coherence	the linking of parts of a text (e.g. paragraphs) so that the text makes sense.	118
cohesion	linking sentences and phrases to create connected text.	117
collocation	the way in which words are used together, e.g. **do** + *the washing up* (not **make + the washing up*).	18
colloquial	conversational, informal.	47
concept question	a question the teacher asks to check that students understand the meaning of new language.	21
connected speech	spoken language in which individual words sometimes link up.	59

consolidation	an activity where students review and integrate the points taught in a lesson or series of lessons. This is often a writing activity at the end of a lesson.	16
consonant	the letters of the English alphabet excluding vowels: *b, c, d, f,* etc.	30
context	the background to and situation in which we hear, read, or use language.	11
contraction	the short form of verbs as used in informal writing. An apostrophe is used to represent the missing letter(s), e.g. *Where's Harry? He's gone to London—he'll be back tomorrow.*	60
controlled practice	a form of practice which focuses on the target language and is designed to provide maximum repetition with minimum error.	13
correction code	a set of symbols and letters used by a teacher to mark the kinds of error in a learner's written work: 'S' for spelling error, etc.	121
diagnostic test	a test intended to find out gaps a student's knowledge.	141
dictation	an activity in which a text is read out loud and the learners write it down as accurately as possible.	60
discrete item test	a test which tests understanding of specific language points, e.g. when to use *a* and when to use *the.*	142
drill	teacher-led, repetitive, oral practice to give students pronunciation practice.	13
elicit	asking learners to provide a response. The response could be part of an exchange *(Would you like to have lunch?—I'd love to.),* provide information *(What's the capital of South Korea?—Seoul.),* and so on.	21
ELT	English Language Teaching.	7
error	inaccurate form or use of language.	151
exponent	the way a function is expressed, e.g. *Would you like to…?* is an exponent for making an offer.	32
extensive reading	reading a long text such as a short book or reader for pleasure, with attention to overall meaning. Compare **intensive reading**.	96
extrinsic	relating to external factors such as social pressure, or institutional requirements (examinations and qualifications).	4
feedback	response to what learners say and do.	14, 150
fluency	producing spoken language without unnecessary pauses, false starts, or repetition.	21

focus on form	clarifying how language structures are formed.	13
free practice	practice activities where learners have more choice of the language they use and the aim is to develop fluency; also known as **Production**.	15
function	what we do with language, e.g. apologize, explain.	32
gap fill	an activity in which learners are asked to provide individual words missing in a text.	21
genre-based writing	teaching learners how to produce a particular text type, or genre (e.g. a thank you letter, a business report, or an article), by providing an example text and helping the learners to notice the structure of the text and the language typical to the genre.	118
gist	the general ideas of a text.	78
grading	the order in which things are usually organised in a syllabus, from the simplest to the more complex.	22
group work	a practice activity involving three or more learners.	146
idiom	a group of words with a figurative meaning e.g. *a mountain of work* means 'a lot of work'.	46
idiomatic	idiomatic language uses idioms and so cannot be interpreted literally.	46
information gap activity	a pair or group work activity where students have different information which they must share in order to complete a task.	15
integrated skills	describes classroom activities which combine a variety of language skills.	137
intrinsic	relating to internal factors such as wishes and desires.	4
integrative test	an activity which tests many areas of language at once (vocabulary, collocation, and grammar points, as well as pronunciation and fluency in the case of speaking tasks).	142
intensive reading	reading a short text with attention to detail. Compare **extensive reading**.	96
interaction pattern	the ways in which learners and teacher communicate with each other, e.g. pairs, groups, whole class.	146
intonation	the way a speaker's voice falls or rises to show meaning and emotion.	60
input	language read or heard by learners.	10
jazz chant	a short rhyme or chant with a strong beat, used to help learners get used to the contractions of connected speech.	60

kinaesthetic learning style	learning best when using movement.	5
lead-in (warm up)	activity used at the beginning of a lesson to get the learners' attention, stimulate their interest and curiosity, and start them thinking and speaking in English.	11
lexical item	a piece of vocabulary; can be a word or a phrase.	45
lexical set	a group of words that all relate to the same topic e.g. *dress, hat,* and *shirt* are all members of the lexical set *clothing*.	46
lexis	the words and phrases of a particular language.	46
linker	a word which links ideas in a sentence, e.g. *and, but, moreover*.	94
mind map	a diagram used to show ideas linked to a theme, with the theme placed at the centre and the ideas around it.	56
mingling activities	information gap activities where the whole class interact informally.	114, 146
minimal pair	two words with one difference in sound, e.g. *hit/ heat, road/ load, hat/ hut*.	58
monitor	to listen to the students to check their use of the language.	40
narrative	a description of a series of events.	99
object	in the sentence *He was wearing a sweater*, the noun phrase *a sweater* is the object or direct object. The object usually comes after the verb.	19
pair work	an activity involving two learners practising a particular skill or a language item.	34
peer correction	one learner correcting another. Compare **self-correction**.	152
phoneme	the individual sounds in a language are its *phonemes*.	58
phonetic script	a system of symbols used in written text to represent **phonemes**.	58
phrasal verb	a verb + adverb combination, e.g. *I **got up** early; Did you **turn off** the heating?*	45
placement test	a test given to students at the beginning of a course to determine their language level and which class is best for them. Compare **progress test** and **diagnostic test**.	141
PPP	stands for presentation–practice–production: a lesson model based on target language presented at the beginning of the lesson.	16
prefix	an affix at the beginning of a word to change its meaning, e.g. *in**accurate***. Compare **suffix**.	46

presentation	first focus on new language items, intended to clarify form and function.	12
process writing	dividing the writing activity into stages, each of which practises a subskill.	118, 120
production	See **free practice**.	15
productive skills	writing and speaking: the skills which involve language production rather than internal response to language.	72
productive vocabulary	vocabulary which a learner can produce when speaking or writing.	45
proficiency test	a test which will show how good a student is at using or understanding language.	141
progress test	a test given during a course to see how far a learner's language ability has improved. Compare **diagnostic test** and **placement test**.	141
pyramid discussion	a discussion technique in which learners discuss questions working in groups of first two, then four, then eight learners.	106
realia	real objects such as packaging, magazines, objects, stamps, etc.	47
recast	to correct a learner's error by repeating it but with the correct form.	21
receptive skills	reading and listening: the skills which involve internal response to language rather than language production.	72
receptive vocabulary	vocabulary which a learner can understand by listening or reading but cannot produce readily in speaking and/or writing.	45
recycle/review	to revise things previously studied and relate them to what is being currently studied.	22, 140
register	variation in style in which a person speaks or writes depending on the formality of the situation.	47
remedial work	work designed to help learners overcome gaps and errors in their English.	22
role play	an activity in which learners take on different parts and act out a situation.	34
scanning	reading a text quickly to find specific information.	92
scheme of work	a teaching plan for a series of lessons.	137
schwa	the phonetic symbol /ə/ used to show an unstressed vowel.	60

self-access centre	a room with resources that the students can use for autonomous learning.	153
self-correction	when a student corrects his or her own mistakes either spontaneously or with direction and support from the teacher.	151
simulation	a particular type of role play where the students take on roles in a location.	34
skill	each of the four major modes of communication—reading, writing, listening, and speaking. See **receptive skills** and **productive skills**.	72
skimming	reading a text quickly to get the general idea or gist.	92
stress	where the emphasis is placed on a word or sentence when speaking, e.g. the first syllable of *telephone* is stressed — /ˈtələfəʊn/. An example of sentence stress is *I **love** you*.	59
STT	student talking time: class time dedicated to the learners talking, as opposed to the teacher.	146
subject	in the sentence *The ship sails in an hour*, the noun phrase *the ship* is the subject.	19
substitution drill/ substitution practice	a teacher-controlled form of practice where the teacher gets the learners to produce sentences of the same grammatical structure with some elements changed, e.g. *My **jacket** is about two years old; My **watch** is about two years old.*	13
substitution table	an illustration on the blackboard of a grammatical pattern, showing the elements that can be substituted. Compare **substitution drill**.	13
suffix	letters added to the end of a word to change its function, e.g. *happily*. Compare **prefix**.	46
syllable	a unit of speech which can be made up of a single vowel, e.g. *a*, or a combination of vowels and consonants, e.g. *cough*.	29
syllabus	a plan or programme for a course, specifying content, sequence, and often methodology.	22
synonym	a word that has a similar meaning to another, e.g. *quick* and *fast*.	47
target language	the language that learners are aiming to learn. In a lesson plan, this may be a structure, a function, or lexis.	11
task	an activity which has a purpose (other than that of using the target language) and an outcome, e.g. doing a class survey of leisure activities to find out the most popular pastime.	17

(TBL) task-based learning	a lesson sequence centred around a task or series of tasks that the students carry out.	17
test–teach–test	a lesson in which students are first given a task to carry out unaided to see how well they can do it (test). This is followed by language input (teach) and practice and then by repetition of the task or a similar task (test).	17
text	an example of the target language. These can be spoken texts —conversations, speeches, quotes, and so on—or written texts —a newspaper article, a short story, a report, a composition, etc.	12
transcript	a written copy of a spoken text (generally used after a listening task).	12
TTT	teacher talking time: class time where the teacher is talking, usually giving instructions, giving feedback, etc.	146
verb	in the sentence *The parcel arrived yesterday*, the word *arrived* is a verb. Verbs are words like *make, talk, expect, carry, discover*. There are also the auxiliary verbs *be, have*, and *do* and modal verbs, e.g. *can, should*.	19
visual learning style	learning best when using visual material such as pictures, diagrams, or writing.	5
vowel	*a, e, i, o, u*; the English alphabet contains five vowels. Compare **consonant**.	30
warm-up	See **lead-in**.	11
weak form	a weak form is produced when a vowel sound like the /æ/ sound in *have* is not stressed, as in the sentence **How** many **sisters** have you **got**?	60
word field	a group of words related to the same topic, e.g. *carbon emissions, ozone layer, polluting, increasing* might all be part of the word-field *environment*.	46

Acknowledgements

Some of these definitions are taken or adapted from
Success in English Teaching, Learning and Teaching English,
and *Oxford Learner's Grammar.*

Grammar terminology table

Noun	A word such as *desk, apple,* or *information* which can follow the word *the*.
proper noun and common noun	A proper noun is a name, e.g. *Jessica, New York*. It begins with a capital letter and does not normally have a determiner such as *a* or *the*. Other nouns are **common nouns**, e.g. *table, business, mistake, treatment*.
collective noun	A noun referring to a group, e.g. *audience, class, gang, team*.
compound noun	These are nouns made up of more than one word, e.g. *town hall, football match*. Sometimes the words are written together, e.g. *girlfriend*.
countable noun	A countable noun can be either singular or plural and can be used with *a/an*, e.g. *a **bag**, three **hours**, some **trees***. See also **uncountable noun**.
uncountable noun	These are nouns like *flour, equipment, advice,* that cannot be counted and have no plural form.
noun phrase	A group of words that functions as a noun, e.g. ***The café we went to last night** was lovely.*
Pronoun	Pronouns stand for nouns, e.g. instead of ***John** saw the cat* we can write, e.g. ***He** saw the cat.*
subject pronoun	*I, you, he, she, it, we, you, they* are subject pronouns, e.g. ***I** love you.*
object pronoun	*me, you, him, her, it, us, you, them* are object pronouns, e.g. *I love **you**.*
possessive pronoun	*Mine, yours, his, hers, its, ours, yours, theirs* are possessive pronouns, e.g. *That coat is **mine**.*
reflexive pronoun	*Myself yourself himself herself itself ourselves yourselves themselves*, e.g. *I made it **myself**.*
relative pronoun	*who, whom, which, where, that* are relative pronouns, e.g. *A choreographer is a person **who** creates dance routines.*
Verb	In the sentence *The parcel arrived yesterday*, the word *arrived* is a verb. Verbs are words like *make, talk, expect, carry, discover*.
main verb	A main verb carries the main meaning in a sentence, e.g. *I **clean** my teeth twice a day.*
auxiliary verb	These are the verbs *do, have,* and *be* which are added to main verbs to make a question, e.g. ***Do** you want to go swimming?*, a negative, e.g. *I **don't** think so*, different aspects of the verb, e.g. ***Has** anybody seen my pen?*, the passive, e.g. *The accident **was reported** in the papers*, and emphatic forms, e.g. *She **does** talk about him a lot.*

modal verb	The modal verbs are *can, could, must, need, should, ought, may, might, will, would*, and *shall*, e.g. *I **can** drive; We **should** support the idea*. A modal verb always has the same form.
transitive verb	A verb that has an object, e.g. *We **enjoyed** the meal; The postman **brings** the letters*.
intransitive verb	An intransitive verb cannot have an object, e.g. *The parcel **arrived**. It can have an adverb or adverbial phrase after it, e.g. *The police **appeared** eventually; Let's **go** to the park*.
verb tense and aspect	The tense is a form of the verb which shows whether we are talking about the present, e.g. *I **play**, he **knows**, we are*, or the past, e.g. *I **played**, he **knew**, we **were***. The various combinations of tense and aspect can also be called tenses, e.g. *I have played* is the present perfect tense.
passive and active	A passive sentence has a verb form with *be* and a past participle, e.g. *My coat **was stolen**; The windows **are being cleaned***. Compare the active sentences *Someone stole my coat* and *We're cleaning the windows*.
regular verb and irregular verb	A regular verb is the same as most others: it follows the normal pattern. The verb *call* has a regular past tense and past participle *called*, but the verb *sing* has an irregular past tense and past participle: *sing, sang, sung*.
participle	The past participle is used after *have* in perfect tenses, e.g. *They have **arrived**; How long has he **known**?* The present participle is the *-ing* form of the verb, e.g. *walking, eating*, used after *be* in the continuous, e.g. *I was **working***, and in other structures, e.g. *He lay on the bed **reading***.
gerund	The *-ing* form of the verb used like a noun, e.g. ***Sailing** is fun; I've given up **smoking***.
infinitive	The infinitive is the base form of the verb, e.g. *They let us **stay** the night*. We often use it with *to*, e.g. *They invited us **to stay** the night*, and the to-infinitive is often used after an adjective (e.g. *It's good **to see** you*), after certain verbs, and to express purpose (e.g. *I came here **to see** you*).
phrasal verb	A phrasal verb is a verb + adverb combination, e.g. *I **got up** early; Did you **turn off** the heating?*
Adjective	An adjective is a word like *big, new, special, famous*, used to describe something.
comparative adjective	An adjective form with *-er* or *more* used to compare one thing with another, e.g. *My ice cream is **bigger** than yours; This chair is **more comfortable** than that one*.

superlative adjective	An adjective form with *-est* or *the most* used to make a comparison, e.g. *This is **the biggest** ice cream I've ever seen; Which is **the most comfortable** chair of these three?*
Adverb	In the sentence *The time passed **slowly***, the word *slowly* is an adverb. Adverbs express ideas such as how, when, or where something happens, or how true something is.
adverb of time	*early, late, in the morning,* etc. e.g *She got up **late** after the party.*
adverb of place	*in, on, under, between, opposite, in front of,* etc. e.g. *There are lots of cows **in** the countryside.*
adverb of manner	*happily, sadly, quickly, terribly,* etc. e.g. *She smiled **happily**.* Common irregular forms include *She dances **well*** (not **goodly*); *He runs very **fast*** (not **fastly*).
adverb of frequency	*always, often, sometimes, never, usually, hardly ever,* etc. e.g. *The news is **always** on TV at 10pm at home.*
adverb of degree	*extremely, very, fairly,* etc. e.g. *That film was **extremely** funny.*
adverbial phrase	An adverb phrase is either an adverb on its own, e.g. *carefully, often,* or an adverb which is modified by an adverb of degree, e.g. *very carefully, more often.*
Preposition	A preposition is a word like *on, to, by,* or *with*. It is usually followed by a noun phrase, e.g. ***on** the water, **to** the left.*
Preposition of time	*in, on, at,* etc. e.g. ***on** Monday, **at** the weekend, **in** July.*
Preposition of place	*in, on, in front of, behind, next to,* etc. e.g. *The children are playing **behind** the trees.*
Preposition of movement	*across, along, into out of,* etc. e.g. *Never run **across** the road.*
other	*For, with, of,* etc. e.g. *Come **with** me.*
Prepositional phrase	A prepositional phrase is a preposition + noun phrase, e.g. ***in the studio; from Australia,*** or a preposition + adverb, e.g. ***since then**.* It often functions as an adverbial phrase, e.g. *I've got an interview **on Thursday**.*

Determiner	A word that can come before a noun to form a noun phrase, e.g. *a photo*, ***the*** *result*, ***my*** *old friend*, ***this*** *week*.
definite article	The word *the*.
indefinite article	The word *a* or *an*.
quantifier	A word that says how many or how much, e.g. ***all*** *the books*, ***some*** *milk*, ***half*** *of the students*, ***enough*** *money*.
demonstrative	*this, that, these,* and *those* are demonstrative determiners or pronouns, e.g. *I like **this** building more than **that** one.*
possessive	The words *my, your, his, her, its, our, your, their* used before a noun, e.g. ***my*** *flat*, ***her*** *name*.
Conjunction	A word such as *and, but, because, when,* or *that*, which links two clauses, e.g. *I believe **that** it's true.*

Acknowledgement

Some of these definitions are taken or adapted from *Oxford Learner's Grammar*.

Further reading

1 Some Basic Principles

Harmer, J. 1998. *How to Teach English.* Harlow: Pearson Education.

Harmer, J. 2007. *The Practice of English Language Teaching, Fourth edition.* Harlow: Pearson Education.

Lindsay, C., and **P. Knight.** 2006. *Learning and Teaching English.* Oxford: Oxford University Press.

Willis, D., and **J. Willis.** 2007. *Doing Task-based Teaching.* Oxford: Oxford University Press.

Teaching English in low technology environments

Baker, J., and **H. Westrup,** 2000. *The English Language Teacher's Handbook - How to Teach Large Classes with Few Resources.* Continuum.

Dobbs, J. 2001. *Using the Board in the Language Classroom.* Cambridge: Cambridge University Press.

Nolasco, R,. and **L. Arthur.** 1988. *Large Classes.* London: Macmillan.

Wright, A. 1984. *1000+ Pictures for Teachers to Copy.* Harlow: Pearson Education.

2 Focus on Language

2.1 The structure of a language lesson

see references under 'Some Basic Principles'

2.2 Focus on grammar

GRAMMAR REFERENCE

Coe, N., M. Harrison, and **K. Paterson.** 2006. *Oxford Practice Grammar (Basic).* Oxford: Oxford University Press.

Eastwood, J. 2005. *Oxford Learner's Grammar.* Oxford: Oxford University Press.

Eastwood, J. 2006. *Oxford Practice Grammar (Intermediate).* Oxford: Oxford University Press.

Swan, M. 2005. *Practical English Usage. Third Edition.* Oxford: Oxford University Press.

Swan, M. and **D. Baker.** 2008. *Grammar Scan: Diagnostic tests for Practical English Usage, third edition.* Oxford: Oxford University Press.

Thornbury, S. 1997. *About Language.* Cambridge: Cambridge University Press.

Yule, G. 2006. *Oxford Practice Grammar (Advanced).* Oxford: Oxford University Press.

CLASSROOM ACTIVITIES AND IDEAS

Hall, N., and **J. Shepheard.** 1991. *The Anti-Grammar Grammar Book.* Harlow: Pearson Education.

Scrivener, J. 2003. *Teaching Grammar.* Oxford: Oxford University Press.

Thornbury, S. 1999. *How to Teach Grammar.* Harlow: Pearson Education.

Rinvolucri, M., and **P. Davis,** 1995. *More Grammar Games.* Cambridge: Cambridge University Press.

2.3 Focus on functions

see titles listed under 'Some basic principles'

2.4 Focus on vocabulary

BACKGROUND READING

Thornbury, S. 2002. *How to Teach Vocabulary.* Harlow: Pearson Education.

DICTIONARIES

Oxford Advanced Learner's Dictionary, Seventh Edition. 2005. Oxford: Oxford University Press.

Oxford Wordpower Dictionary, Third edition. 2006. Oxford: Oxford University Press.

SELF STUDY MATERIALS

Gairns, R. and **S. Redman.** 2008. *Oxford Word Skills—Basic.* Oxford: Oxford University Press.

CLASSROOM ACTIVITIES AND IDEAS

Gairns, R., and **S. Redman..** 1986. *Working with Words.* Cambridge: Cambridge University Press.

Hadfield, J. 1998. *Elementary Vocabulary Games.* Harlow: Pearson Education .

Hadfield, J. 1999. *Intermediate Vocabulary Games.* Pearson Education.

Morgan, J., and **M. Rinvolucri.** 2004. *Vocabulary, Second edition.* Oxford: Oxford University Press.

2.5 Focus on pronunciation

BACKGROUND READING.

Kelly, G. 2004. *How to Teach Pronunciation.* Harlow: Pearson Education.

Underhill, A. 2005. *Sound Foundations, Second edition.* London: Macmillan.

CLASSROOM ACTIVITIES AND IDEAS

Graham, C. 2000. *Jazz Chants Old and New.* Oxford: Oxford University Press.

Hancock, M. 1995. *Pronunciation Games.* Cambridge: Cambridge University Press.

Hewings, M., and P. Ur. 2004. *Pronunciation Practice Activities.* Cambridge: Cambridge University Press.

Laroy, C. 1995. *Pronunciation.* Oxford: Oxford University Press.

O'Connor, J.D., and C. Fletcher. 1989. *Sounds English: A Pronunciation Practice Book.* Harlow: Pearson Education.

3 Focus on skills

3.1 The structure of a skills lesson

see titles listed under 'Some basic principles'

3.2 Listening

BACKGROUND READING

Ur, P. 1984. *Teaching Listening Comprehension.* Cambridge: Cambridge University Press.

CLASSROOM ACTIVITIES AND IDEAS

Hadfield, J., and C. Hadfield. 1999. *Simple Listening Activities.* Oxford: Oxford University Press.

White, G. 1998. *Listening.* Oxford: Oxford University Press.

3.3 Reading

Background Reading

Grellet, F. 1981. *Developing Reading Skills* Cambridge: Cambridge University Press.

Nuttall, C. 1982. *Teaching Reading Skills in a Foreign Language.* London: Macmillan.

CLASSROOM ACTIVITIES AND IDEAS

Bamford, J., and R. Day. 2004. *Extensive Reading Activities for Teaching Language.* Cambridge: Cambridge University Press.

Hadfield, J., and C. Hadfield. 2000. *Simple Reading Activities.* Oxford: Oxford University Press.

3.4 Speaking

BACKGROUND READING

Maley, A. 1982. *Drama Techniques in Language Teaching, Second edition.* Cambridge: Cambridge University Press.

Thornbury, S. 2005. *How to Teach Speaking.* Harlow: Pearson Education.

CLASSROOM ACTIVITIES AND IDEAS

Hadfield, J., and C. Hadfield. 1999. *Simple Speaking Activities.* Oxford: Oxford University Press.

Nolasco, R,. and L. Arthur. 1987. *Conversation.* Oxford: Oxford University Press.

Porter Ladousse, G. 1987. *Role Play.* Oxford: Oxford University Press.

Ur, P. 1981. *Discussions that Work.* Cambridge: Cambridge University Press.

3.5 Writing

BACKGROUND READING

Harmer, J. 2004. *How to Teach Writing.* Harlow: Longman.

CLASSROOM ACTIVITIES AND IDEAS

Hadfield, J., and C. Hadfield. 2000. *Simple Writing Activities.* Oxford: Oxford University Press.

Hedge, T. 2005. *Writing, Second Edition.* Oxford: Oxford University Press.

4 Putting it together

4.1 Planning lessons and lesson sequences

Woodward, T. 2001. *Planning Lessons and Courses.* Cambridge: Cambridge University Press.

4.2 Review, assessment, and remedial work

Masden, H. 1983. *Techniques in Testing.* Oxford: Oxford University Press.

4.3 Classroom management

Dörnyei, Z. and **T. Murphey.** 2003. *Group Dynamics in the Language Classroom.* Cambridge: Cambridge University Press.

Gardner, B., and **F. Gardner.** 2000. *Classroom English.* Oxford: Oxford University Press.

Hadfield, J. 1992. *Classroom Dynamics.* Oxford: Oxford University Press.

Hughes, G.S. 1981. *A Handbook of Classroom English.* Oxford: Oxford University Press.